Christmas TRADITIONS

LEISURE ARTS, INC.
Little Rock, Arkansas

EDITORIAL STAFF

Managing Editor: Susan White Sullivan
Designer Relations Director: Debra Nettles
Craft Publications Director: Deb Moore
Special Projects Director: Susan Frantz Wiles
Senior Prepress Director: Mark Hawkins
Senior Technical Writer: Laura Siar Holyfield
Technical Associate: Christina Kirkendoll
Editorial Writer: Susan McManus Johnson
Foods Editor: Jane Kenner Prather
Contributing Test Kitchen: Rose Glass Klein
Design Captain and Lead Photostylist: Lori Wenger
Designers and Photostylists: Kim Hamblin,
 Kelly Reider, Anne Pulliam Stocks, and Becky Werle
Art Publications Director: Rhonda Shelby
Art Category Manager: Lora Puls
Lead Graphic Artist: Amy R. Temple
Graphic Artists: Dayle Carozza, Janie Wright,
 and Jeanne Zaffarano
Photography Manager: Katherine Atchison
Imaging Technicians: Brian Hall, Stephanie Johnson,
 and Mark R. Potter
Publishing Systems Administrator: Becky Riddle
Publishing Systems Assistants: Clint Hanson and
 John Rose

BUSINESS STAFF

Vice President and Chief Operations Officer:
 Tom Siebenmorgen
Corporate Planning and Development Director:
 Laticia Mull Dittrich
Vice President, Sales and Marketing: Pam Stebbins
National Accounts Director: Martha Adams
Sales and Services Director: Margaret Reinold
Information Technology Director: Hermine Linz
Controller: Laura Ogle
Vice President, Operations: Jim Dittrich
Comptroller, Operations: Rob Thieme
Retail Customer Service Manager: Stan Raynor
Print Production Manager: Fred F. Pruss

Library of Congress Catalog Number 2008921828   Hardcover ISBN 1-60140-832-3

10 9 8 7 6 5 4 3 2 1

Whether your Christmas is already filled with treasured family customs or you are just starting to celebrate on your own, this collection of exciting ideas will help you build lasting memories of this special season.

Created because we know the traditions of Christmas are what bring the holiday—and our loved ones—nearer to us each year, every page of this beautiful book features meaningful ways to enrich your holiday experience. Create gifts destined to become treasured keepsakes. Make decorations that evoke tender memories. The unforgettable recipes and easy designs for entertaining will ensure that your parties and family get-togethers will have a special place on everyone's calendar for years to come.

As you read the personal stories from our readers and editors, we know you will be touched and inspired—just as we were as we worked on this, our heartfelt Christmas gift to you.

Merry Christmas, now and always.

Table of
Contents

Decorate
page 46

Add meaning to your holiday décor, now and forever.

Celebrate
page 110

Special occasions to keep every December.

Treasure

More than any other time of the year, Christmas is full of opportunities to observe our families' unique traditions. And whether it's the hanging of a wreath at the door, the selection of the almost-perfect tree, or mailing a mile-high stack of Christmas cards, your family counts on the annual reappearance of their favorites to signal the official beginning of the holidays.

It's not really Christmas, until the family treasures come down from the attic.

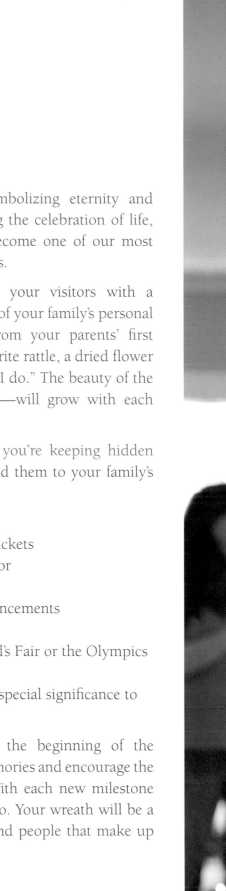

With its circular shape symbolizing eternity and evergreen branches signifying the celebration of life, the Christmas wreath has become one of our most enduring Christmas traditions.

Welcome the holidays and your visitors with a wreath decorated in symbols of your family's personal milestones—a ticket stub from your parents' first date, your middle child's favorite rattle, a dried flower from the day you both said, "I do." The beauty of the wreath—and its significance—will grow with each passing year.

Think about the mementos you're keeping hidden away. Bring them out and add them to your family's Keepsake Wreath:

Old Christmas Ornaments
Railway Passes and Ship Tickets
Granddad's Pocket Watch or
    Grandmother's Brooch
Birth and Wedding Announcements
Military Service Medals
A Souvenir from the World's Fair or the Olympics
ID Tags from Family Pets
Any small item that holds special significance to
    your family

Unpacking your wreath at the beginning of the holiday season will spark memories and encourage the retelling of family stories. With each new milestone passed, add another memento. Your wreath will be a small history of the events and people that make up your family.

Remember...

there are no real rules for the holiday wreath. Whether you choose a more orthodox, evergreen wreath—or defy convention with a different type or shape, let your wreath reflect your family's style and personality.

Keepsake Wreath
Instructions are on page 37.

9

Whatever your age, the anticipation of the arrival of Christmas is contagious. Only fifteen more days until Santa comes! In ten days everyone will be gathered together again! Just five more days to finish all the preparations! As the house fills with the sounds and fragrances of the upcoming holiday, the excitement grows. In all the flurry and fuss, it's easy to lose sight of the meaning of Christmas.

Make the countdown part of your family's annual Christmas tradition. When the final block of this calendar is turned, a simple reminder of the season is revealed—a silhouette of the world's most important family, sharing the world's first-ever Christmas.

Advent Calendar
Christmas is here, and your family marked each day of Advent with a new tradition—a calendar made of purchased wood blocks and a frame. Instructions are on page 36.

Wish List Box
Instructions are on page 37.

12

I want a race car and I want a radio and a space ship and candy.

Wishes will always be a big part of the Christmas tradition—and not just for the children. While the little ones may wish for their heart's desire, grownups are happy just seeing their children's dreams come true. The latter is easier with a little help from Santa and his magic Wish Box. After Thanksgiving, help each child write his Christmas list and tuck it into the box for Santa to magically read—all the way from the North Pole! These lists will become keepsakes your family will enjoy reading again each year.

Begin a *New* Tradition

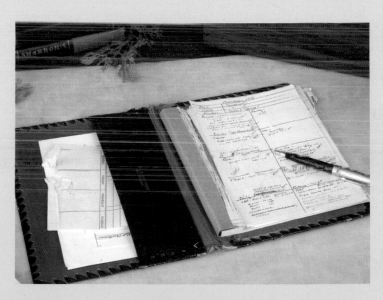

When we were small children, my father began a family tradition that I hope we will always observe. Every year, right after we've finished having Thanksgiving dinner, he brings out an old leather-bound journal. And suddenly, the room is full of children—old and young alike. This journal has come to be called the Wish Notebook, and Dad uses it to record what everyone (adults, too) would like for Christmas. There's always a lot of laughter and teasing as he asks for and then writes down all our holiday wishes.

The notebook has become a sign to us that Christmas is on its way again. But it's also a family history, of sorts. My daughter can see what I wished for when I was her age and get a glimpse of the girl I used to be. My mother's wishes when she was my age sound an awful lot like the woman I have become. Turning back the pages to see what we asked for in the past has become as much a tradition as recording each year's wishes. It gives us insight into who we were and how much we've grown and changed over the years.

Anne Stocks
Little Rock, Arkansas

13

Christmas Card Tote
Instructions are on page 38.
Make two, in case you want to
give one away.

If, despite the technological alternatives, Christmas cards and letters have remained a part of your yearly tradition, you already know the reasons why. In the time it takes to form the letters, to think carefully about a turn of phrase, to address the envelopes and affix the stamps, the communication has already begun. Slowing down to think about the addressee, to imagine her face as she opens your letter or hear his chuckle when he reads your card, you may even feel as though you were right there with them.

If you've let this tried and true practice fall to the wayside in the rush to get everything done during the Christmas season, maybe you'd like to slow down and reacquaint yourself with the pleasures and intimacy of hand writing your holiday correspondence. Make it a real occasion with a portable tote for cards, stationery, stamps, address book, and pens, and your conversation can begin wherever you are.

Remember...
during the Christmas season, buying postage online will help you avoid standing in Post Office lines. These days, you can even personalize your stamps with family photos!

15

No matter how busy our everyday lives, many of us try to pause for a moment at Christmastime to reconnect via a photo card, and someone, somewhere, can't wait to receive it.

A Christmas photo card with news of the family is even more important these days—now that brothers and sisters live a continent's span apart. And if you are one of the lucky families who exchange these special cards, you already know how hard it is to pack them away after the holidays are over.

An extra-special tabbed photo card box is perfect for keeping up with the Joneses. And the Moores and Martins, too.

Christmas Photo Card Box
Instructions are on page 39.

Begin a *New* Tradition

When my children were still in elementary school, we lost all our Christmas decorations to a basement flood. That year, the only decorations were those we made. So one rainy Saturday afternoon in December, the whole family sat down to make felt stockings. My husband cut out the patterns and I sewed them together on the machine. The children decorated their stockings with felt scraps, sequins, yarn, and buttons as they saw fit.

The following year, my youngest son began asking to make Christmas stockings again. Every year since, we get together as a family on the first Saturday of December to make that year's stockings. Naturally, I've saved them all; the children enjoy comparing their more recent, accomplished efforts with childish attempts from the previous years (and of course, with each other's).

Now that they are all teenagers, my kids are sometimes too busy for some family activities, but this is one they still make time for.

Kay Powell
Providence, Rhode Island

Felt Stockings
Instructions are on page 40.

Santa's Elf Boxes
For hiding little gifts. Instructions are on page 40.

Begin a *New* Tradition

When my aunt Donna was a child, the holiday decorations would magically appear in her home shortly after Thanksgiving Day. Donna's mother explained that this was done by a Christmas elf, who was also watching Donna and reporting back to Santa on her behavior.

Years later, Donna decided that Santa needed to assign a Christmas elf to her young sons, Joel and Lyle.

Sixtus Bagdesarian was an important member of Santa's correspondence team. It was Sixtus's job to write each boy a letter in early December, informing the children that he was helping Santa keep score on who was being naughty or nice. If the boys would leave their wish lists for Sixtus, the elf would make certain Santa received them.

Throughout December, more notes from the elf showed up in lunch boxes, desk drawers, and under pillows, each encouraging the boys to be good and to remember those less fortunate.

Finally, on Christmas Eve, one small gift from Sixtus would appear in each boy's room. Along with the gift was a final note praising their deportment. The next morning, the children would wake up to find everything from their wish lists.

I believe any family would truly enjoy having their own Christmas elf. What a wonderful way to create cherished memories while keeping kids entertained until Christmas!

Mary Hutcheson
Little Rock, Arkansas

Elf Note
Via Christmas tree bough delivery.
Instructions are on page 41.

Dear Hanna,

With a box and a bow,
All sprinkled in snow,
And a wish for your highest cheer,
I present you a prize
Of the best kind and size,
You've been really good this year.

This brief list of long-standing national and international charities highlights just a few that either concentrate their efforts on specific areas of need during the Christmas season, or make it easier for you to contribute during the holidays. Some will even provide you with a donor gift card that you can present to your loved one. Information about the work done by these organizations and how you can contribute is readily found on their Websites.

Heifer Project International
www.heifer.org

Make a Wish International
www.worldwish.org

Oxfam
www.oxfam.org

Samaritan's Purse
www.samaritanspurse.org

Toys for Tots
www.toysfortots.org

WorldVision
www.worldvision.org

Since tales of wealthy Saint Nicholas's legendary Christmas generosity began circulating centuries ago, charity has been an important part of the season. Today, if the people on your list already have everything they need and most of what they want, part of your holiday tradition each year may be to donate to others in their names.

Just because you are helping someone you might not know, doesn't mean that your gift is any less personal. You can still share the experience of the perfectly presented gift, all wrapped up in the spirit of the season. Enclose your charitable announcement in a handmade gift card and your friend or family member will know that you were thinking of them—as well as others with urgent needs—this holiday season.

Charity Card Keeper
Instructions are on page 42.

Confused about how to choose a charity?

CharityNavigator.org is a free online service that provides evaluations for thousands of charitable organizations. Their *Frequently Asked Questions for Donors* page explains what kind of charities they evaluate and how to use the Website. Helpful graphs show the actual percentage of funds going to program, administrative, and fundraising expenses, and you'll also see a ratings comparison chart showing your chosen charity alongside similar organizations.

Wrapping Caddy
With everything in one place, the whole family can find what they need. Instructions are on page 43.

Holiday Wish List

Begin a *New* Tradition

In a family as large as ours, it's just too much for Mom to do all the gift wrapping. When I was seven months pregnant with my sixth child, I happened upon a gift wrapping system by necessity that has since become a tradition my children look forward to every year.

That year, I recruited all the kids to help get me through the mound of unwrapped packages and gifts. The kids wrapped and decorated the presents in shifts, while I marked what was wrapped on a list. I had them rotate so they couldn't see their own gifts and they only got to see a couple gifts for each person. They loved it! They guarded the secrets well—although they did enjoy the old "I know what you're getting" routine.

I enjoyed watching the clumsy attempts of wrapping by the little ones, the gentle help offered by the older ones, and the creativity they all put into it. Some of the gifts looked like they were mangled, but it only added to the charm. I wouldn't want perfectly wrapped gifts if it meant losing the precious look of joy on their faces as they announced, "Look, Mom, I did it!"

Audra Silva
Pendleton, Oregon

The keeping of secrets is a long-held Christmas tradition. Starting this year, recruit every member of the family as co-conspirators in the holiday intrigue. Hidden behind closed doors after supper or on Saturday afternoon, the rustle of paper and the whisper of gift-giving secrets can be a wonderful opportunity to make a special connection with each individual child, your daughter-in-law, or your husband—and for them to enjoy uninterrupted time alone with you. A little paper and a bit of ribbon are all you'll need to make these small moments together momentous and memorable.

To make gift wrapping easier for everyone, keep everything in one convenient, easy-on-the-eyes location. This mobile gift wrap center holds all the paper, bags, tags, ribbon, tape, and other supplies needed for pretty packages

When you were a girl, you could hardly wait for her Christmas visits because you thought she was the coolest grownup around. She always remembered the name of the boy you liked, shared sodas with you after midnight, and could be counted on to keep a confidence. You wanted to be just like her when you grew up.

This year, say "Welcome" to your favorite aunt with a new tradition. A breakfast menu card like the ones used at fine hotels will show her how special she still is to you.

Guest Room Menu
Take the guesswork out of the morning meal while telling holiday visitors you have their comfort in mind.
Instructions are on page 44.

Aunt Sarah

☐ *Swedish Pancakes*

☐ *Blueberry Pancakes*

☐ *Eggs Benedict*

☐ *Scrambled Eggs*

☐ *Fresh Fruit with Devonshire Cream*

☐ *Breakfast Casserole*

☐ *Banana Nut Muffin*

☐ *Strawberry Muffin*

☐ *Cinnamon Bread*

Swedish Pancakes

    2   cups milk
    2   eggs
 1½   tablespoons sugar
  ¼   teaspoon salt
 1½   cups all-purpose flour
    4   tablespoons butter
        Garnish: Sweetened
          Whipped Cream
          (recipe on page 121),
          fresh strawberries and
          blueberries, and
          powdered sugar

Whisk first four ingredients together. Add flour, ½ cup at a time, to milk mixture, whisking until smooth. Melt butter in a small skillet or crepe pan; cool. Whisk butter into milk mixture. For each pancake, pour about ½ cup batter into the hot pan, tilting pan until batter covers the bottom of pan. Turn pancake over when lightly browned. Place on waxed paper to cool. (Pancakes can be frozen between layers of waxed paper.)

To serve, roll up pancakes and garnish with whipped cream, fresh fruit, and powdered sugar, if desired.
Yield: about 21 six-inch pancakes

Devonshire Cream
Delicious served with fresh fruit or scones.

    1   package (3 ounces) cream
          cheese, softened
  ½   cup whipping cream
  ¼   cup powdered sugar
  ¼   teaspoon vanilla extract

Beat cream cheese and whipping cream until mixture is smooth. Stir in powdered sugar and vanilla. Serve with fresh fruit or scones.
Yield: about ¾ cup cream

Eggs Benedict with Hollandaise Sauce

    2   English muffins, split in half horizontally
    8   slices Canadian bacon
    4   poached eggs
        Hollandaise Sauce (recipe follows)

Place English muffins on a baking sheet; top each muffin half with 2 slices Canadian bacon. Bake at 350° for 10 to 15 minutes or until bacon is hot and muffins are toasted. Place each muffin on a serving plate and top with a poached egg and Hollandaise Sauce. Serve immediately.
Yield: 4 servings

Hollandaise Sauce
    3   egg yolks
  ⅛   teaspoon cayenne pepper
  ¼   teaspoon salt
  ½   cup butter, room temperature, cut into 1 tablespoon pieces, and divided
 1½   tablespoons lemon juice

Place egg yolks, cayenne pepper, salt, and 3 tablespoons butter in the top of a double boiler over simmering water. Gradually add lemon juice, stirring until mixture begins to thicken. Add remaining butter, a tablespoon at a time, stirring constantly until sauce is thickened. Serve immediately.
Yield: ¾ cup sauce

Swedish Pancakes

Speedy Spinach Lasagna

1 3/4 cups water
1 can (8 ounces) tomato sauce
1 can (6 ounces) tomato paste
1 package (1.37 ounces) spaghetti sauce mix
2 eggs
1 container (15 ounces) ricotta cheese
1 package (10 ounces) frozen chopped spinach, thawed and drained
1/2 cup grated Parmesan cheese, divided
1/2 teaspoon salt
1 package (8 ounces) lasagna noodles, uncooked, broken in half, and divided
2 cups shredded mozzarella cheese, divided

Whisk water, tomato sauce, tomato paste, and spaghetti sauce mix in a saucepan over medium heat until heated through; remove from heat. Beat eggs in a large bowl. Beat in ricotta cheese, spinach, 1/4 cup Parmesan cheese, and salt. Cover the bottom of a lightly greased 13 x 9-inch baking dish with sauce. Layer half the noodles, half cheese mixture, half mozzarella, and half remaining tomato sauce mixture. Repeat layers. Sprinkle top with the remaining 1/4 cup Parmesan cheese. Cover dish with greased aluminum foil. Bake at 350° for 1 hour; remove foil and bake 15 more minutes or until cheese is melted and bubbly. Let stand 10 minutes before serving.
Yield: 8 servings

To make ahead: After assembling, lasagna can be frozen up to one month. Allow to thaw in refrigerator and bake as directed above.

Taco Soup

An easy soup that freezes well. Keep in the freezer for those last-minute holiday dinners.

1 pound ground chuck or sausage
1 large onion, chopped
1 can (15 ounces) black beans or pinto beans
1 can (15 ounces) chili beans
1 can (14.5 ounces) stewed tomatoes
1 can (10 ounces) tomatoes with green chiles
1 package (1.5 ounces) dry taco seasoning mix
1 package (0.7 ounce) dry Italian dressing mix
Garnish: sour cream and shredded Cheddar cheese

Cook meat and onion in a large skillet until meat is brown and onion is transparent. Stir in remaining ingredients. Cover and simmer on medium-low heat 20 minutes or until heated through, stirring occasionally. Garnish with sour cream and shredded Cheddar cheese, if desired.
Yield: 10 cups soup

To make ahead: After adding all ingredients, soup may be frozen up to one month. Allow to thaw in refrigerator and simmer in a covered saucepan for 30 minutes.

Begin a New Tradition

Christmas shopping at our house is serious business. We really enjoy the adventure of braving the crowds to shop the Day-After-Thanksgiving sales. Dressed for speed, we hit the stores in the wee hours of the morning, and everyone tries really hard to get all our shopping finished before crying, "Uncle."

After a day like that, nobody wants to cook, but my bunch has never been big on turkey leftovers. So, I make sure there's something hearty and already cooked waiting for us when we get home. I make a main dish as much as a month ahead and store it in the freezer. Other family members bring side dishes just for this meal. Laughing over tales of the "one that got away" and recounting the antics of the other shoppers over a warm meal brings us all closer together and inspires us to plan for next year.

Jo Myers
Reston, Virginia

Few of us can see a Christmas cookie without thinking of Mom. Whether the cookie was rolled and cut or dropped by the spoonful, she made sure we had a job on the cookie line that was perfectly suited to our special kitchen skills.

As the years have gone by, we've added new cookie recipes to our collections—a cousin's special fruitcake bars, a best friend's mint-frosted brownies. We enjoy these treats even more because they remind us of these special people. And we know the recipes we share with others will also remind them of us.

Remember...
Christmas isn't a
season. It's a feeling.
Edna Ferber

Christmas Cookies
Share the homemade joy. Instructions for the Cookie Gift Tin
are on page 44. Cookie recipes are on pages 32 and 33.

Begin a *New* Tradition

The first Christmas after I moved into my own apartment, my wish list was filled with items I needed for my new kitchen. My mom, though, knew exactly what I needed.

In the weeks before Christmas she called on all the greatest cooks on both sides of the family with an urgent SOS. That Christmas morning, I received a beautiful, hand-rubbed wooden recipe box filled with the secrets to my favorite childhood dishes as cooked by my mother, grandmothers and great-grandmothers.

I cried when I opened it. Even a novice cook like me understands that food is love.

Hannah Moore
Conway, Arkansas

Gingerbread Cookies

- 1/2 cup shortening
- 1/2 cup sugar
- 1/2 cup dark molasses
- 1/4 cup water
- 2 1/2 cups all-purpose flour
- 1 teaspoon cinnamon
- 1 teaspoon ground ginger
- 1/2 teaspoon baking soda
- 1/4 teaspoon ground cloves
- 1/4 teaspoon salt
- 1 cup powdered sugar
- 2 teaspoons water

Cream shortening and sugar. Blend in molasses and water. In a separate bowl, combine flour, cinnamon, ginger, baking soda, cloves, and salt. Add dry ingredients to molasses mixture. Cover and chill 2 hours.

Preheat oven to 375°. Roll dough 1/8" thick on a lightly floured surface. Use a 3 1/2"-high gingerbread boy cookie cutter to cut out dough. Bake on ungreased baking sheets for 8 to 10 minutes. Cool completely.

Combine powdered sugar and water. Transfer to a pastry bag fitted with a small round tip. Outline cookies with icing and use icing to attach silver dragées (dragées are for decorative use only; remove before eating cookie).

Yield: about 2 dozen cookies

Sugar Cookies

- 1/2 cup butter, softened
- 1/2 cup margarine, softened
- 1 1/2 cups powdered sugar
- 1 egg
- 1 1/2 teaspoons vanilla extract
- 3/4 teaspoon almond extract
- 2 1/2 cups all-purpose flour
- 1 teaspoon baking soda
- 1 teaspoon cream of tartar
  light brown decorating sugar

Beat together butter, margarine, powdered sugar, egg, and extracts. In a separate bowl, combine flour, baking soda, and cream of tartar. Stir flour mixture into butter mixture. Cover and chill 2 to 3 hours.

Preheat oven to 375°. Divide dough in half. Roll each half 1/8" thick on a lightly floured surface. Cut out dough using a star-shaped cookie cutter (ours was 3" wide). Sprinkle with brown decorating sugar (see note). Bake for 5 to 7 minutes or until lightly browned on edges.

Note: To make star-shape decorations on cookies, draw around cookie cutter on white paper. Reduce to 80% on a photocopier. Trace pattern onto acetate sheet; cut out star stencil. Place stencil on cookie and sprinkle with brown sugar. Lift stencil straight up.

Yield: 3 1/2 dozen cookies

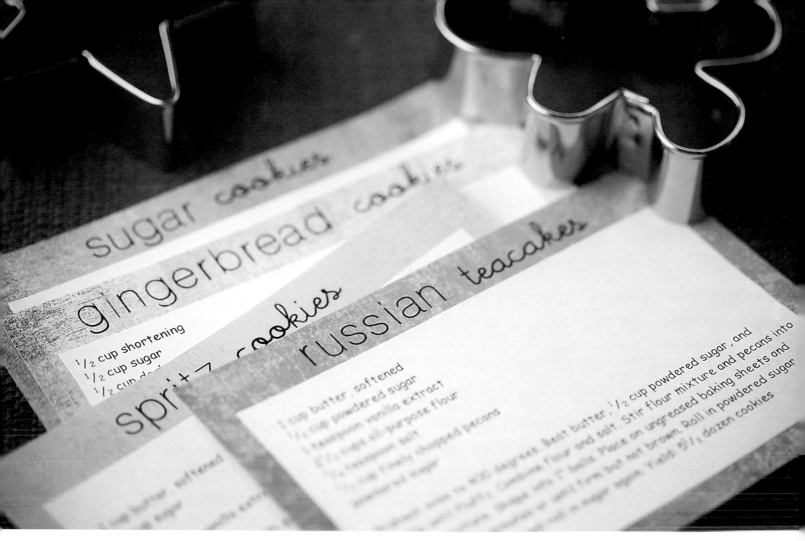

Spritz Cookies

 1 cup butter, softened
$^1/_2$ cup sugar
 1 egg
 1 teaspoon vanilla extract
$2^1/_2$ cups all-purpose flour
$^1/_2$ teaspoon salt
$^1/_2$ teaspoon baking powder
$^1/_2$ teaspoon nutmeg

Preheat oven to 400°. Beat butter and sugar until fluffy. Beat in egg and vanilla. In a separate bowl, combine remaining ingredients; stir into butter mixture. Fit a cookie press with a tree plate and fill press with $^1/_4$ of the dough at a time. Form shapes on ungreased baking sheets. Decorate with gold dragées (dragées are for decorative use only; remove before eating cookie). Bake for 3 to 5 minutes or until set but not brown.
Yield: 6 dozen cookies

Russian Teacakes

 1 cup butter, softened
$^1/_2$ cup powdered sugar
 1 teaspoon vanilla extract
$2^1/_4$ cups all-purpose flour
$^1/_4$ teaspoon salt
$^1/_2$ cup finely chopped pecans
    powdered sugar

Preheat oven to 400°. Beat butter, $^1/_2$ cup powdered sugar, and vanilla until fluffy. Combine flour and salt. Stir flour mixture and pecans into butter mixture. Shape into 1" balls. Place on ungreased baking sheets and bake for 8 to 10 minutes or until firm but not brown. Roll in additional powdered sugar while warm. Cool and roll in sugar again.
Yield: $5^1/_2$ dozen cookies

Remember . . .

cushion cookies for crumble-free shipping. Place wax paper between layers and packing material in the spaces around cookies. Dry-popped popcorn and crumbled, unsalted rice cakes make good fillers.

Dark Chocolate-Cherry Cookies

- 1 package (12 ounces) dark chocolate chips
- 3/4 cup butter
- 3/4 cup firmly packed brown sugar
- 2 eggs
- 1 teaspoon vanilla extract
- 1/2 cup all-purpose flour
- 1/4 teaspoon baking powder
- 1 package (5.5 ounces) dried cherries

Place chocolate chips and butter in a microwave-safe bowl and microwave on HIGH for 2 minutes. Stir until mixture is smooth. Stir in brown sugar, eggs, and vanilla until well blended. In a separate bowl, combine flour and baking powder; add to chocolate mixture. Stir in cherries. Drop about 1/4 cupfuls of dough onto an ungreased cookie sheet. Bake at 350° for 12 to 14 minutes. Cool 1 minute and transfer to wire racks to cool completely.

Yield: about 1 1/2 dozen cookies

All-Dressed-Up Cookie Boxes
Instructions are on page 45.

Every family has one—the tried-and-true cookie, cake, or candy that only makes an appearance at Christmas. These holiday treats have become such a fixture that many families wouldn't dream of having Christmas without them. If you're responsible for one of these culinary institutions, by all means, give it the presentation it deserves.

A hand-painted, one-of-a-kind platter is the perfect way to present your one-of-a-kind treats. The local do-it-yourself pottery studio will host your painting activities and kiln-fire your piece for you. Even if your favorites are traveling by box, don't send them out of the house until they're all buttoned up and ready to go. Make these simple sleeves to dress up plain white treat boxes.

Painted Plate
The perfect home for the perfect cookie. Instructions are on page 45.

Advent Calendar

(from pages 10 and 11)
Turn over a block each day
in December to reveal a
classic nativity silhouette
(turn all of the top row over
on the 1st and the bottom
row on the 24th). We
included patterns for two
sides of the blocks to make
the advent calendar.

Sand the blocks as needed
to fit in the shadow box.
Paint one side of each
block metallic green
(allow each coat of paint
to dry thoroughly before applying additional coats). Paint the
remaining sides randomly with green acrylics and metallic
green. With metallic sides down, arrange the blocks in the
shadow box. Stamp the numbers 1–24 on the four middle
rows of blocks. Enlarge the patterns (page 149) to 159%, and
transfer holly leaves and berries onto the blocks as desired.
Paint the leaves metallic gold and shade with burnt umber.
Paint the berries metallic red. Highlight the leaves and berries
with pearl. Flip the blocks to the reverse side. Transfer the
enlarged nativity pattern onto the center blocks. Remove
the blocks from the shadow box and paint the nativity black.
Apply two to three coats of black paint to the frame. (If you'd
like to make yours a six-sided puzzle, paint or decoupage
images on the remaining sides of the blocks.) Apply sealer to
the blocks and frame.

• medium-grit sandpaper • thirty-six 2" square wood blocks
• wooden shadow box with a 12" x 12" opening • green, gold,
and red metallic paints • burnt umber, pearl, black, and three
shades of green acrylic paints • paintbrushes • number rubber
stamps • black StazOn™ ink pad • transfer paper • clear
acrylic matte sealer

Keepsake Wreath

(from page 9)

Adorn a magnolia wreath with cherished memorabilia. Begin by wiring three groupings of glass balls to the wreath along with silver and glittery gold berry picks. Intersperse meaningful tags and trinkets among the leaves. (Cut tags from tissue-covered cardstock and add decorative paper, rub-on messages, mementos, or pieces of jewelry.) Enjoy adding a new memory to your wreath for each family milestone.

Wish List Box

(from page 12)

Send Santa your wishes via this magical box.

1. Remove the front latch from the box. Glue the letters onto the box lid. Fill in the seams between the letters and the lid with wood putty (smooth with your finger or a palette knife). Allow the putty to dry.

2. Lightly sand, then paint the box red. Enlarge the damask pattern (page 149) as desired and cut out the desired elements (we copied ours at 142%). Arrange and draw around the designs on the lid and sides, freehanding between the letters. Using two to three coats, paint the damask pattern dark red.

3. Brush Mod Podge on the tops of the letters and sprinkle with glitter. Shake off the excess onto the paper plate.

4. Enlarge the word "list" (ours is at 142%) and transfer it onto the lid. Draw over the word with the paint pen. Apply sealer to the box. Replace the latch.

• wooden box with hinged lid (ours is 8$1/2$"w x 8$1/4$"h x 1$1/2$"d) • wood glue • wooden letters (ours are 4"h) • wood putty • palette knife (optional) • fine-grit sandpaper • red and dark red acrylic paint • paintbrush • Mod Podge® • clear glitter • paper plate • transfer paper • silver paint pen • clear acrylic matte spray sealer

Christmas Card Tote

(from page 14)

With this handy tote nestled beside your favorite chair, preparing your holiday cards each year will seem effortless. Use a $1/2$" seam allowance except where noted.

1. Cut one 12" x 23" front/back piece and two $7^1/2$" x $8^1/4$" ends each from tote fabric, lining, and interfacing.

2. For stability, baste interfacing to the wrong side of each tote piece, using a $3/8$" seam allowance. Matching right sides and raw edges, pin one long edge of the front/back piece to one end piece (Fig. 1). Sew the pieces together, stopping $1/2$" from the corner (shown by a dot on Fig. 2). With the needle in the fabric, pivot, then sew across the bottom to the remaining dot. Pivot and sew the remaining edge. Repeat to sew the opposite end to the front/back. Turn the tote right side out.

3. Cut two 3" x 12" handles from tote fabric. For each handle, matching right sides, sew the long edges together. Turn right side out and press. Matching right sides and raw edges, center and pin the handles to the tote front and back leaving 3" between the handle ends.

4. For the pocket, cut a $5^3/4$" x 6" piece from the tote fabric. Press the top long edge $1/2$" to the wrong side; topstitch $3/8$" from the fold. Sew ribbon on the front of the pocket, covering the stitching.

5. Press the raw edges of the pocket $1/4$" to the wrong side. Center and pin the pocket to the lining front/back, with the top of the pocket $2^1/2$" from one short edge of the lining. To add penholder loops, fold four 3" ribbon lengths in half and pin the ends under the pocket sides near the top and bottom. Use a $1/8$" seam allowance to sew the pocket in place.

6. Leaving an opening at the bottom of one end for turning, sew the lining front/back to the ends; do not turn right side out. Matching right sides, insert the tote in the lining. Sew the tote and lining together along the top edge. Turn right side out and sew the opening closed. Tuck the lining in the tote. Topstitch $1/2$" from the top edge. Glue ribbon over the topstitching on the tote and lining.

- $3/4$ yd each of tote fabric, lining fabric, and heavyweight interfacing • 3 yds of $3/8$"w red velvet ribbon • fabric glue

Fig. 1

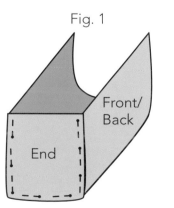

End

Front/Back

Fig. 2

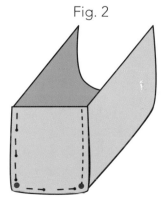

Christmas Photo Card Box

(from page 17)

This terrific organizer for holiday photo cards gives you easy access to photos you've received from friends and family members through the years.

1. Insert a layered scrapbook paper and vellum label (we rubbed the word, "Photos" on ours) in the label holder on the box front. Line the inside lid with paper and glue 1½"w ribbon at the back and front, looping the front end for a clever handle.

2. Enlarge the tabbed divider patterns (page 151) to 221%. Using the large pattern, cut nine heavy-cardstock dividers and add alphabet rub-ons (cut three each with a left, center, and right tab). Using the small pattern, cut a cardstock divider for each family whose photo cards you receive, and write their family name on the tab.

3. To make the ribbon snowflake base, knot each end of three ⅛" x 4½" ribbon lengths and glue them together (Fig. 1). For each branch, follow Fig. 2 to fold a 5" ribbon length, gluing where shown in blue. Fold three 1¼" ribbon lengths in half. Tuck and glue the ends of one branch in each fold (Fig. 3). Alternating branch styles, glue each branch to the base and the bead to the center. Glue the end of one branch to the top of the box.

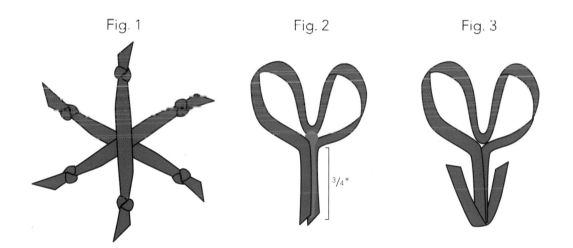

| Fig. 1 | Fig. 2 | Fig. 3 |

¾"

• scrapbook paper • vellum • vellum tape • rub-on alphabets • 8¼"w x 11¾"d x 6¼"h photo box with label holder • double-stick tape • fabric glue • ⅛"w and 1½"w ribbons • heavy cardstock or illustration board • contrasting cardstock • fine-point permanent pen • pearl bead

Felt Stockings

(from page 19)

Sew the stockings together ahead of time for each family member and enjoy an afternoon of sharing and creativity.

1. For each stocking, enlarge the pattern (page 153) to 200% and cut the stocking from a doubled 10" x 28" felt piece. Cut a 1/2" x 5" felt hanger. Fold the hanger in half and pin the ends between the stocking front and back. Leaving the top open, zigzag the stocking pieces together.
2. Use purchased felt shapes or letters, cut out your own felt designs, or cut pieces using the enlarged patterns to decorate each stocking. Glue the pieces in place.
3. Add embellishments with fabric glue or embroidery floss.

• felt in assorted colors • felt shapes and letters • tracing paper (optional) • fabric glue • embellishments (we used pom-poms, sequins, rickrack, jingle bells, and velvet ribbon) • embroidery floss

Santa's Elf Boxes

(from page 20)

Make a different-colored box for each member of the family. Remove the shadow box backing and the latch. Use spray adhesive to line the backing with 2"w ribbon. Paint the box and lid and allow to dry. Tie a charm onto 1/4"w ribbon (our charms say, "wish," "believe," and "love"). Placing the charm in the shadow box, reinsert the lid backing. Brush glue on the lid and sprinkle with glitter, shaking the excess onto the paper plate. Replace the latch.

For each box you will need:
• 2 1/2" square wooden box with shadow box lid • spray adhesive
• 2"w ribbon or fabric scrap • acrylic paint • paintbrush • charm
• 1/4"w ribbon • disposable foam brush • craft glue • glitter
• paper plate

Elf Note

(from pages 20 and 21)

Start with a note from your own family's elf and watch the legend unfold through the years.

1. For the note, enlarge the border designs (page 148) to 155%. Transfer the designs onto an 8½" x 11" torn handmade paper piece. Use the fine-point pen to write and personalize the note. Draw over the corners and leaves with paint pens and emboss the swirls. Add dots of glue and glitter for the berries. Drip sealing wax on a looped piece of ⅛"w satin ribbon and seal it with your elf's initial.

2. For the cover, place two 4" x 8" ribbon lengths side by side, overlapping long edges by ¾"; zigzag the ribbons together. Cut a 6¼" x 8" piece each of interfacing and green fabric. Center the interfacing, then fabric right side up on the wrong side of the ribbon base. Press the long edges of the ribbon ½" to the front of the fabric and topstitch along the ribbon edges. Match right sides and use a ½" seam allowance to sew the short ends together to form a tube. Turn the cover right side out.

3. To embellish the cover, fasten brads through holes pierced along the seam. Wire the bell, ⅛"w silk ribbons, and hanger to the center brad. Slip the cover over the rolled-up note.

• transfer paper • handmade paper • black fine-point permanent pen • gold and green paint pens • embossing ink • gold embossing powder • embossing heat tool • craft glue • red glitter • sealing wax and initial seal • ⅛"w satin ribbon • 4"w red silk ribbon • medium weight interfacing • green shimmery fabric • silver brads • large needle • fine-gauge silver wire • wire cutters • silver jingle bell • 4" lengths of ⅛"w red and green silk ribbons • silver swirl ornament hanger

Charity Card Keeper

(from pages 22 and 23)

Donate to a charity in honor of someone you love and tuck the card in the pocket of this clever card keeper.

1. Fold the short ends of a 6" x 12" cardstock piece to meet in the center. Cut a 6" green print paper square in half and tape the pieces over the outside flaps.

2. Open the card keeper and tape a red print paper pocket to the inside. Add a rub-on message to the pocket and insert the donation card. Center and punch two holes ¼" apart near the edge of the right flap.

3. Cut two 2¼"-long velvet leaves. Gather and sew the leaves together near one end. Tie the button to one end of a 50" floss length and sew it to the flap. Wrap the floss around the card keeper three times, then around the button a few times. Sew the leaves on the floss so the leaf ends tuck under the button. Trim the excess floss.

• green cardstock • green and red print scrapbook papers • double-sided tape • white rub-on alphabets • charity donation card • 1/16" dia. hole punch • green velvet ribbon or fabric scrap • green embroidery floss • 1" dia. red shank button

Wrapping Caddy

(from page 24)

Start with a simple crate found at your local craft store and in no time, you'll have a compact caddy that's easy to tote wherever unwrapped packages are hiding.

1. Turn the crate on end and remove a top slat to leave space for the wrapping paper rolls to poke through as shown in Fig. 1. (Though your crate may not look just like ours, you can still remove a slat from one spot and add it to another to create compartments for your papers and sacks.)

2. Trim one end of the removed slat so it just fits inside the crate, and glue it to the new bottom, about halfway from the front (Fig. 2).

3. Cut one dowel 2" wider than the crate and cut two dowels the outside width of the crate. Drill sets of $1/2$" dia. holes through the sides for dowel placement (the long dowel A holds rolls of ribbon, dowel B holds tissue paper, and dowel C supports boxes and gift sacks—use our measurements in Fig. 3 or customize the placement to suit your needs).

4. Sand the crate. Glue the second and third dowels in place. Fill in the ends with wood putty, let dry, and lightly sand.

5. Prime, then paint the crate. Stencil the sides. Apply wood tone spray to the crate.

6. Add silver tape along the crate edges and around the ends of the long dowel. Pre-drill a $1/16$" dia. hole and insert a tack in each end of the dowel. Hot glue a notepad to one side of the caddy and add hangers for tags, scissors, or tape.

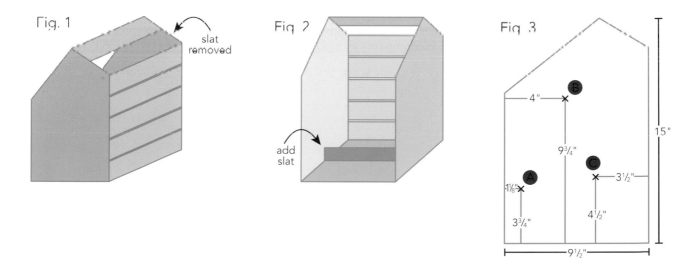

Fig. 1 — slat removed

Fig. 2 — add slat

Fig. 3 — 4", 9³/₄", 15", 3½", 1⅛", 3¾", 4½", 9½"

• wooden vegetable crate with slatted bottom (ours is 14" x 9$1/2$" x 15") • small prying tool or screwdriver • miter saw • wood glue • $3/8$" dia. dowels • drill with $1/16$" and $1/2$" bits • sandpaper • wood putty • primer • paintbrushes • green and dark green acrylic paints • border stencil • glossy wood tone floral spray • silver copper foil tape (used for stained glass) • two decorative silver upholstery tacks • hot glue gun • notepad • adhesive-backed hangers

Guest Room Menu

(from page 26)

Make a holiday guest feel extra special with a personal breakfast menu. (Make several copies and use a new one each day.)

Wrapping excess paper to the back, use glue or spray adhesive to cover the mat board piece with scrapbook paper. Enlarge the pattern (page 150) to 178% and cut a scrapbook paper pocket. Fold and glue the side, then bottom flaps to the back of the menu holder. Print a personalized list of breakfast options for your guest to choose from; trim it to $3^{1}/_{2}$" x 11" and insert it in the pocket. Cut holes on each side of the menu near the top and insert eyelets. Thread a 26" ribbon length through the eyelets. Secure a jingle bell near the ribbon ends with the brad.

• scrapbook paper • craft glue or spray adhesive
• 5" x 12" piece of mat board • craft knife and cutting mat • eyelets and setter • $^{3}/_{8}$"w velvet ribbon
• jingle bell • brad

Cookie Gift Tin

(from page 31)

To make a divider for each tin, cut two foam core rectangles each the height and diameter of the tin's interior. Cutting a slit halfway through the center of each rectangle, intersect the rectangles to form an X. Cover the top edges with silver tape and place the divider in the tin. Add the cookies and close the lid. Freeze up to 6 weeks.

• cookie tin, at least 8" dia. • craft knife and cutting mat • $^{3}/_{8}$"-thick foam core • $^{1}/_{4}$"w silver copper foil tape (used for stained glass)
• assorted cookies

All-Dressed-Up Cookie Boxes

(from page 34)

Wrapping with ribbon is so fun and easy—you'll want to use this idea to trim lots of packages. Cut ribbons long enough to wrap around each cookie-filled box with an inch overlap. Layer and fuse the ribbons together with hem tape and sew or fuse the ends under. Sew button(s) on one end of the ribbon. For each loop closure, knot the ends of an elastic loop together and sew it to the remaining end of the ribbon.

• various-width ribbons • Dark Chocolate-Cherry Cookies in plastic wrap and tissue paper • gift boxes (ours are 4" cubes)
• double-stick hem tape • buttons
• elastic cord

Painted Plate

(from page 35)

Call ahead to your local do-it-yourself pottery store for available sizes of round plates. Draw your own pattern or follow Sizing Patterns (page 158) to enlarge our pattern (page 156) to fit your plate. (We enlarged the pattern to 204% to fit our 11⅝" diameter plate.)

Take the sized pattern and a piece of graphite transfer paper to the studio. Use the ballpoint pen to transfer the pattern to the plate (the lines will disappear when it's fired). Choosing from the wide variety of paints available at the shop, apply several coats for vivid color. Leave the plate at the shop to be fired. When it's ready, fill it with cookies or candy and delight someone special.

• sized pattern • graphite transfer paper • ballpoint pen • plate and paints supplied by the studio

Decorate

We know in our hearts that Christmas is not about the lights or the tinsel. More than anything else, it's the one time of year when the world slows down enough to allow us a moment to enjoy being with family, friends, neighbors, and co-workers. Together, we enjoy sharing the old, established traditions; these well-loved customs and observances help make the holidays, special days. So too, can a new tradition.

Take a moment this holiday season to look for new ways to celebrate being together—making an extra special ornament, hanging a wreath you've made, or creating a centerpiece that speaks to the history of your family. This year, let the holiday decorations at your house reflect everything that is marvelous and memorable about you and yours.

Peacock Feather Wreath
Make fond memories a part
of your holiday tradition.
Instructions are on page 70.

When it comes to observing tradition, old and new ideas can go together as easily as generations gathered around the dinner table. When your new holiday decorations also carry the stamp of your experiences, they become more than just beautiful—they become meaningful. Seize the opportunity to recapture a favorite experience or recount your childhood to your children or grandchildren by introducing elements that carry personal meaning for you, such as this splendid peacock feather wreath.

Begin a *New* Tradition

As a young wife and mother in the 1950s, my mom had plenty on her to-do list every day. It would have been so easy for her to have given us something to keep us occupied and out of her hair. Instead, she regularly gathered us up and took us for an afternoon at the zoo.

My sister, being the adventure seeker she still is today, soon discovered the secret hiding places the peacocks used to escape the crowds. After each visit, she would emerge victorious from behind a bush or beneath the trees with at least one of the birds' lush plumes. Soon, she had filled a large vase with beautiful green and teal feathers, which she kept for many years to come.

So many years later, the sight of a single peacock feather reminds me of my mother's generosity of time to her young daughters. And all over again I admire my sister's fearlessness, enjoy my mother's devotion, and relive the countless afternoons with nothing more pressing on our calendar than paying our respects to the animals.

Susan Sullivan
Little Rock, Arkansas

Holly Canvas
A sprig of holly becomes forever golden. Instructions are on page 71.

This joyous work of art is the backdrop for a happy holiday, and the design is easy to make in any size you choose. Paint a grand design for the mantel or a modest motif for a table or shelf. Just think how proud you'll be to display your composition for many Christmases to come! Bring it out at the start of the season to signal the official beginning of the holidays.

Remember . . .

It isn't so much what's on the table that matters, as what's on the chairs.

William S. Gilbert

Chair Slipcover
The best-dressed seat in the house. Instructions are on page 70.

*E*xtend the seasonal décor beyond the evergreens with rich red accents for the sofa. The easy craft of needle felting embellishes a pair of simple-to-sew pillow slipcovers. Much faster than embroidery, the elegant designs are created by punching the fibers of wool yarn into fabric with a needle tool. Adding the soft luxuries to your holiday may well become your favorite Christmas tradition.

Remember . . .

There is nothing like staying

at home for real comfort.

Jane Austen

Pillow Slipcovers
This and every Christmas season, refresh your throw pillows with needle felted covers. Instructions are on pages 72 and 73.

Elegant Tree Skirt
Fashioned from a plush throw, this tree skirt will add luxury to every Christmas season. Instructions are on page 73.

The sweetest thing about a tradition is the opportunity to pass it on—or to help create a new one. If there are newlyweds in your family, why not invite them to your house to make ornaments? This simple start to gathering their own collection of Christmas decorations will build family bonds and a fond memory of this early time of togetherness.

Remember...

What an enormous magnifier is tradition! How a thing grows in the human memory and in the human imagination, when love, worship, and all that lies in the human heart, are there to encourage it.

Thomas Carlyle

Gold-Leafed Ornament
A papier-mâché ornament can be the basis for building a strong—and lovely—family tradition. Instructions are on page 74.

Home Sweet Home
Create the house you've always wanted.
Instructions are on pages 74–76.

Surely every aspiring baker dreams of creating memorable houses like this—all gingerbread spiciness and frosting sweetness. Now that you've been baking a while, maybe it's time to build this magical cookie cottage. Once it's complete, you'll find yourself wondering why you waited so long to add the longstanding kitchen tradition to your home. You'll also find yourself dreaming of new ways to decorate next year's gingerbread creation!

Begin a *New* Tradition

My daughters and I make Christmas cookies every year. One year, in the middle of our baking, my youngest daughter declared that we simply had to make cutout gingerbread cookies. The problem was, we had no cookie cutters. The disappointment of my beloved child led me to discover you can make cutout cookies without cutters by freehanding your designs in the dough with a knife. This gave us the freedom to be more creative, so we decided it would be fun to make one cookie representing a different family member each year. The kids don't care if the gingerbread person is a bit lopsided. They just have fun spending creative time together as a family.

Merrilee Gasaway
Bryant, Arkansas

Who says stockings have to hang by the chimney? These childhood favorites are just as festive in the window, at the foot of the bed, or on the back of a chair.

If there's a family member who can't be home for Christmas, be sure to hang his or her stocking extra-early to be filled with gifts. Allow plenty of time to ship the filled stocking to its owner with a "Do Not Open Until December 25" tag. Now your loved one can empty a stocking along with the rest of the family, bringing everyone closer in spirit on the big day.

Remember...

Happy, happy Christmas...
that can win us back to the
delusions of our childish days;
that can recall to the old man
the pleasures of his youth;
that can transport the sailor
and the traveler, thousands of
miles away, back to his own
fireside and his quiet home!

Charles Dickens

Cream Silk Stockings
Santa would never put coal in
these silk and velveteen stockings.
Instructions are on page 78.

Appliqué Stockings
Poinsettias—destined
to become heirlooms.
Instructions are on
page 77.

Evergreens, peppermint, oranges, cinnamon, cloves—the scents of the season become a part of your family's memories right along with the color of your decorations and the happy sound of holiday music. Among the many fragrances you can enjoy at Christmas is the heartening scent of paperwhites. These springtime flowers make an exquisite living bouquet, and you don't have to be a gardener to grow them. Forcing bulbs into bloom for Christmastime is a simple tradition that goes back more than a hundred years. You can also grow the scentless amaryllis for its color, and arrange potpourri, herbs, or fresh fruit all around the flowerpot for fragrance. Whatever aromas evoke Christmas for you, just a little planning can combine them into a refreshing sight for the eyes.

Begin a *New* Tradition

In 1969, my mother made a centerpiece to celebrate the arrival of her first grandchildren—my twin sons. There were two of everything: birds, holly sprigs, ribbons, and so forth. For the next twenty-five years, Mom's Christmas table featured that special arrangement.

When she passed away on December 22 of that last year, Mom's centerpiece was already on the table—and it was the first thing I saw as I entered her house that last time. Now, the centerpiece belongs to one of the twins whose birth it commemorated.

Cheryl Gunnells
Little Rock, Arkansas

Fragrant Arrangement
Make a tabletop arrangement that smells as lovely as it looks. Instructions are on page 79.

Paperwhites Arrangement
At Christmas, anyone can have a green thumb.
Instructions are on page 78.

A fast flurry of stenciled snowflakes
turns a glass circle into a table mat
you'll want to display each Christmas.
Instructions are on page 79.

Of course the holidays find you happily dressing the mantel and the dining table, but what about the coffee table? Throughout the year, it's a drop-off point for school books and magazines. It may even be a prop for tired feet when no one's looking. But at Christmas, your coffee table can shine with the joy of the season. Create a centerpiece by arranging candles and roses on a snowflake-stenciled glass mat. Or fashion a trio of golden birds that you can display each year. Still concerned about those wandering feet? Ask Santa for an early gift—a comfy ottoman the whole family can enjoy.

Three French Hens
Cheery chirpers and moss trees bring the outdoors inside. Save the birds to be used again next year. Instructions are on page 80.

Pine Door Spray
Three parts nature, two
parts elegance. Instructions
are on page 81.

When you dress the entryway of your home for the season, do you do so to delight the mail carrier? Perhaps you decorate for the family across the street. Maybe you like the way the lights and greenery inspire a sense of community when viewed alongside the neighbors'. Whatever else motivates your choice of décor, it's your personal tradition to surprise and delight friends and family with your holiday decorations. For example, you may decide to assemble this amazing garland with copper stars, faux greenery, and dried florals. Besides pleasing your loved ones, each glimpse of the garland will give the whole world a chance to share your joy. Or envy your good taste.

Hydrangea Garland
Simple decorative components, sensational
holiday results. Instructions are on page 81.

Welcome Mat
A treat for the eyes, as well as the feet. Instructions are on page 80.

Remember . . .

although your flowerbeds have gone dormant, you can still have
beautiful plants on your porch. Visit your local garden center to
purchase or rent evergreens for the season. The living trees or shrubs
will refresh your entryway and complement your decorations.

66

All the excitement of the Christmas season just naturally spills out of the house and onto the porch. When you hang the wreath on the door and add lights to the landscaping, don't forget the first thing your visitors see as they step inside—a friendly doormat. With Internet shopping becoming a popular way to get goodies for decking the halls and floors, the options for choosing a pleasing seasonal mat are ever-increasing. But did you know there's yet another way to get the perfect outdoor rug? Just paint a coir doormat to create the holiday greeting you want.

Snowflake Ornaments
(from page 46)

Transform unfinished papier-mâché or wooden ornaments into glittery snowflakes. We've made two to get you started.

1. Paint the snowflakes and while wet, sprinkle the two large flakes with glitter. Glue silver beads to the tips of the largest snowflake (run the hanger through the ornament hole and catch the top bead on the hanger). Glue a brooch to the center of the snowflake.

2. Hot glue a beaded berry to each tip of the 4" snowflake. Brush glue on the small snowflake and sprinkle it with micro beads. Allow the glue to dry; then, glue the small flake to the center of the large one. Adhere the remaining brooch to the center with a foam dot.

- ivory acrylic paint • paintbrush • 4" dia. papier-mâché snowflake ornament • 4³/₄" and 2¹/₂" dia. wooden snowflake ornaments
- iridescent glitter • craft glue • 7mm silver beads • ornament hangers
- two snowflake brooches (pinbacks removed) • hot glue gun • micro-beaded berry spray • disposable foam brush • clear micro beads
- adhesive foam dot

Tree Topper

(from page 46)

Can't find a topper to match your tree's color scheme? Here's a fun and simple solution.

1. Stack and glue two foam cups together to form a sturdy base and hot glue foam shapes on top. Insert a pencil in the top shape to form the point.

2. Cover the whole topper with a thin layer of Paperclay, dipping your finger in water and smoothing as you go. Be sure to reinforce each joint with the clay. Sand any rough areas after the clay is completely dry.

3. Paint the topper, and when it's dry, brush on a thin layer of glue and sprinkle it with glitter. For added sparkle, cut beaded berries from a spray and hot glue them around a few of the shapes.

4. Poke four evenly-spaced holes through the base near the bottom. Run two 12" wire lengths through the holes and place the topper on the tree. Wrap the wire ends around the branch to secure.

• craft glue • foam cups and assorted foam shapes • hot glue gun • pencil or skewer • Creative Paperclay® • medium-grit sandpaper • acrylic paints • paintbrush • disposable foam brush • white super fine glitter • wire cutters • white micro-beaded berry spray • large needle • 20-gauge wire

Velveteen Tree Skirt

(from page 46)

Let the rich color and texture of this elegant tree skirt provide a vibrant foundation for your ornament collection. Match right sides and use a 1/2" seam allowance for all sewing unless otherwise noted.

1. Sew two 31 1/2" x 62" skirt fabric pieces together along one long edge. Follow Cutting a Fabric Circle (page 158) and use a 30 1/2" string measurement for the outer cutting line. Remove the tack and use a 2" string measurement for the inner cutting line. Cut through all layers along the drawn lines. Unfold the skirt and cut an opening from the outer edge to the center opening midway between the seams. Repeat to cut the skirt lining.

2. For the cording, follow Continuous Bias Binding (page 159) to cut a 2 1/4" x 195" bias strip from the fabric square. Center a 195" cord length on the wrong side of the bias strip. Matching long edges, fold the strip over the cord. Using a zipper foot, sew next to the cord. Trim the flange to 1/2".

3. Matching raw edges, baste the flange of the cording to the outer edge of the skirt. Leaving an opening for turning, sew the lining to the skirt along all edges. Clip the curves and turn right side out. Sew the opening closed.

• 3 1/2 yds cotton velveteen skirt fabric • string • water-soluble fabric pen • thumbtack • 3 1/2 yds cotton lining fabric • 23" square of silky polyester fabric for binding • 5 1/2 yds of 3/8" dia. cotton cord

Peacock Feather Wreath

(from page 48)

For an absolutely stunning display, start with a wreath that fits your space and add fullness with hot-glued greenery picks. Wire a cluster of blue ornaments to the wreath and frame them with peacock feathers. Tuck in glitter picks. Wire green ornaments to more glitter picks and add them to the arrangement. Make single and multiple ribbon loops with or without tails. Secure the ends with wire and hot glue or wire the loops to the wreath.

• large wreath • hot glue gun • greenery picks • floral wire • wire cutters • glossy blue and matte green ball ornaments • peacock feathers • glitter picks • plaid wire-edged ribbon

• about 2 yds fabric for chair cover • velvet needle board or scraps of heavy velvet for pressing cloths • about 6¼ yds of 1½"w velvet ribbon • straight pins • fresh or faux berry sprigs

Chair Slipcover

(from page 51)

Choose a print fabric that complements the rich velvety ribbon. Match right sides and use a ³/₈" seam allowance unless otherwise noted. Use a velvet needle board or velvet pressing cloths when ironing velvet.

1. Cut a fabric piece the length and width to fit your chair, making sure the back of the cover extends to the bottom of the back-rest (we cut ours a few inches narrower than the chair).

2. Cut two ribbon lengths the width of the fabric. Cut two lengths the length of the fabric plus 2". Matching wrong sides and long edges, press each ribbon in half.

3. With the pressed ribbon edge toward the fabric center, pin one short ribbon length along one short fabric end. Sew the ribbon to the fabric. Press the seam allowance to the back. Repeat for the opposite end.

4. Trimming to fit as needed, fold and pin the ends of the long ribbons ¼" to the wrong side and pin the ribbons along the long fabric edges with the pressed ribbon edges toward the center. Sew the ribbons to the fabric and press the seam allowances to the back. Topstitch around the cover along the fabric edges.

5. Cut four 12" ribbon ties. Covering the seat and chair back, place the slipcover over the chair, allowing the excess to drape over the back. Mark tie placement on the front and back with pins and remove the cover. Press one end of each tie ½" to the wrong side and sew the pressed end to the wrong side of the cover where marked. Replace the cover on the chair. Add berry sprigs as you knot the ties.

Holly Canvas

(from page 50)

This piece of art will look tailor-made to fit your home, because it is! Choose a canvas that fits your space and enlarge the design to match. Because metallic paint is thin, apply two or more coats of paint as desired.

1. Choose one of the following options to size and transfer the design.

   Option A. Use a dry-erase marker to trace the pattern onto a transparency sheet. Transfer the design to the canvas using a pencil and an overhead projector. (Craft stores carry inexpensive projectors, or you can use one at a local library.)

   Option B. Refer to the Size Chart (below) or read Sizing Patterns (page 158) to enlarge the pattern (page 155) on a photocopier to the size you need. (The copy store clerk can also help with sizing and proportion.) Tape the pieces together; then, transfer the design onto the canvas with transfer paper, extending pattern lines if needed.

   Option C. Instead of enlarging the entire design, enlarge a few of the leaves and berries on a copier, cut them out, and use a pencil to draw around them on the canvas where you wish.

2. Draw over the pattern lines with the paint pen.

3. Paint the berries bronze, working quickly to blend the bronze with light creamy gold for highlights. (Use a little extender if desired, to keep the paint wet longer.)

4. Paint the canvas background green.

5. Paint the leaves cream and pearl, shading the outer edges and veins with bronze. Allow to dry. Draw over the detail lines with the paint pen as desired.

6. Apply varnish to the canvas.

Some Standard Canvas Sizes	Enlarge to	Enlarge Again to
20" x 24"	388%	—
24" x 30"	400%	121%
30" x 36"	400%	146%
30" x 40"	400%	162%
36" x 48"	400%	194%

• large pre-stretched artist's canvas (ours is 36" x 48") • dry-erase marker and transparency sheet (optional) or graphite transfer paper (optional) • gold paint pen • bronze, light creamy gold, green, cream, and pearl metallic acrylic paints • paintbrushes • paint extender (optional) • acrylic varnish

Pillow Slipcovers

(from page 53)

It's easy to needle felt slip covers for your everyday pillows or to create pillows the size you want, using yarns and fabrics that match your décor. Our instructions are for new pillows—to cover existing pillows, read Sizing Patterns (page 158) and adjust the measurements as needed.

Square Cover for a 16" Pillow

Match raw edges and use a 1/2" seam allowance unless otherwise noted.

1. Choose a computer font and print the initial to use as a pattern (ours is 3" x 5").
2. Cut a 23" square pillow front. Enlarge the pattern (page 154) to 231%. Tape the pattern and pillow front on the light table or window and use the fabric pen to trace the design onto the center of the pillow front. Trace the initial pattern in the center of the design. Place the pillow front inside the hoop.
3. Follow step 2 from the Rectangular Cover to needle felt the design.
4. Trim the pillow front to a 17" square. Baste a 17" muslin square to the back of the pillow front.
5. To make cording, press one end of a 1³/₄" x 72" strip of velveteen fabric 1/2" to the wrong side (this strip will need to be pieced). Beginning 1/2" from the pressed end, center the cord on the wrong side of the strip. Matching long edges, fold the strip over the cord. Using a zipper foot, sew next to the cord. Trim the flange to 1/2".

6. Beginning and ending 2" from the cording ends, baste the flange of the cording around the pillow front. Trimming to fit, insert the unfinished cord end into the folded end of the cording and finish basting.
7. Cut two 11" x 17" velveteen pieces. Fold and pin one long edge of each piece 1/2" to the wrong side; topstitch. Sew three 2" buttonholes along one hemmed edge. Place the pillow front right side up. Matching right sides, place the buttonhole piece on the pillow front. With the hemmed edges overlapping, place the remaining back piece on top and pin all layers together. Sew the front and back together, trim the corners, and turn right side out. Cover the buttons with velveteen and sew them to the pillow back. Insert the pillow form. Sew a tassel to each corner.

• ²/₃ yd linen fabric for pillow front • transparent removable tape • light table or sunny window • water-soluble fabric pen • embroidery hoop • felting needle tool and mat • wool yarn • sweater depiller • 1/2 yd muslin • 1/2 yd velveteen fabric for cording and pillow back • 2 yds of 1/4" dia. cotton cord • three 2" dia. self-covered buttons • 16" square pillow form • 4 tassels

Rectangular Cover for a 12" x 16" Pillow

(from page 53)

Match raw edges and use a 1/2" seam allowance unless otherwise noted.

1. Cut a 17" x 19" pillow front. Enlarge the pattern (page 154) to 229%. Tape the pattern and pillow front on the light table or window and use the fabric pen to trace the design onto the center of the pillow front. Place the pillow front inside the hoop.

2. Refer to Needle Felting (page 159) and follow the felting needle package instructions to attach the yarn to the pillow front with the felting needle tool. Work around the outer edges of the design; then, go back and fill in to give the appearance of crewel needlework. When adding more yarn, overlap the ends to give the yarn a seamless look. When finished, use the depiller to clean up the yarn area.

3. Trim the pillow front to 13" x 17". Baste a 13" x 17" muslin piece to the back of the pillow front.

4. Cut two 11" x 13" velveteen pieces. Fold and pin one long edge of each piece 1/2" to the wrong side; topstitch. Sew a 2" buttonhole near the center of one hemmed edge. Place the pillow front right side up. Matching right sides, place the buttonhole piece on the pillow front. With the hemmed edges overlapping, place the remaining back piece on top and pin all layers together. Sew the front and back together, trim the corners, and turn right side out. Cover the button with velveteen and sew it to the pillow back. Insert the pillow form. Whipstitch trim around the pillow, covering the seam.

• 1/2 yd linen fabric for pillow front • transparent removable tape • light table or sunny window
• water-soluble fabric pen • embroidery hoop • felting needle tool and mat • wool yarn • sweater depiller • 1/3 yd muslin • 1/3 yd velveteen fabric for pillow back • 2" dia. self-covered button
• 12" x 16" pillow form • 1 2/3 yds of trim

Elegant Tree Skirt

(from page 54)

Take pictures while you work or they won't believe you made this luxurious tasseled tree skirt from a faux mink throw and wooden beads.

1. Cut a slit from the center of one side to the middle of the throw. Cut a tree-trunk-size circle from the middle. Hem the cut edges.

2. For each tassel topper, paint the wooden pieces. Aligning the holes, glue a doll pin stand, large bead, and small bead together. Glue ribbon around the topper below the large bead.

3. For each tassel, place a 10" piece of ribbon along the top edge of the cardboard square. Wrap ribbons and fibers around and around the square and the 10" ribbon (we wrapped ours 20 times). Tie the 10" piece tightly around the wound ribbons and fibers. Cut the loops opposite the tie. Thread the tie through the tassel topper and knot close to the top bead. Sew a tassel to each corner of the tree skirt.

• faux mink throw (ours is 52" x 60") • metallic acrylic paint
• paintbrush • 4 wooden doll pin stands • 4 each of 1/2" and 1 1/2" dia. wooden beads • craft glue • assorted ribbons and fibers
• 5 1/2" cardboard square

Gold-Leafed Ornament

(from page 55)

Craft a set of ornaments just like ours, or adapt the technique to work with other shapes or paint colors. Here are the steps we took. Paint the ornament brown and let it dry. Apply liquid adhesive, then gold leaf, to the top and bottom. Lightly sand the edges of the gold leaf. Squeeze small dabs of glaze and each paint color separately on the palette. Dip the small round brush into the glaze, then the gold. Loosely brush the ornament, leaving streaks and brushing onto the edges of the gold leaf. Without cleaning the brush, dip it in glaze and brown paint. Brush the mixture on the ornament. After the glaze mixture dries, add a coat of clear glaze. Tie a ribbon hanger to the ornament.

• brown and gold acrylic paints • paintbrush • papier-mâché ornament • gold leaf with liquid adhesive • fine-grit sandpaper • Krylon® Triple-Thick Crystal Clear Glaze • palette or foam plate • small round brush • velvet ribbon

Gingerbread House

(from page 56)

Here's a fun project for the whole family. Make the house as elaborate or as simple as you wish, but be sure to make cookies from the extra dough to eat while you build it!

Gingerbread

To make a house the size of ours (15"w x 15"h x 8"d), you will need to make 3 recipes of dough.

1 cup butter, softened	1 tablespoon ground ginger
1 cup firmly packed brown sugar	1 teaspoon baking soda
1 cup molasses	1 teaspoon ground cloves
2 eggs	1 teaspoon salt
6 cups all-purpose flour	1 teaspoon ground allspice
1 tablespoon ground cinnamon	1/2 teaspoon baking powder

Cream butter and brown sugar until fluffy in a large bowl. Beat in molasses and eggs. Combine remaining ingredients in another large bowl. Stir dry ingredients into creamed mixture. Divide dough in half and wrap in plastic wrap; chill one hour. (When finished, you will have 6 balls of wrapped dough from the 3 recipes.)

Working with one ball of dough at a time, roll out dough on a lightly floured surface to ⅛"
thickness. For large pieces, roll out dough directly on pieces of parchment paper and then transfer
the paper to your baking sheets. Roll out small pieces on a lightly floured surface and transfer to
ungreased or parchment-covered baking sheets. (Remove and save excess dough.)

  Follow the diagrams (below) to cut out the pieces from dough (make templates from poster
board if you like). Sizes of square and rectangular shapes are labeled on the House diagram.
Irregular pieces have separate diagrams. Trim the sides, chimney, the sides of the chimney top, the
octagonal window, the porch columns, and the door as shown, cutting away the shaded areas. Bake
at 350° for 6 to 15 minutes (depending on the size of your pieces—the pieces should be firm to the
touch when done). Allow large pieces to remain on baking sheets until cool. Transfer small pieces
onto a wire rack to cool.

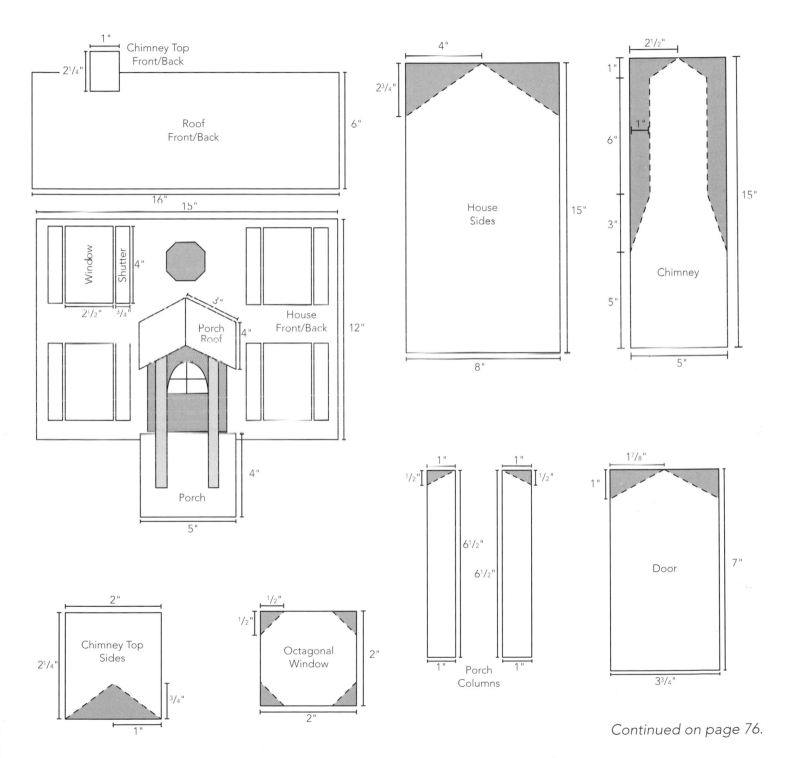

Continued on page 76.

75

 Royal Icing
For a house our size, make 5 recipes of icing. Keep it tightly covered to prevent drying.

2 tablespoons meringue powder
4 cups (one pound) powdered sugar
6 tablespoons warm water
    Pastry bags with small, medium, and large
        decorating tips (#3, #4, and #5)

Beat meringue powder, powdered sugar, and water in a medium bowl at high speed with an electric mixer 7 to 10 minutes or until stiff. Spoon into a pastry bag fitted with suggested decorating tips (refill bag as necessary).

Fig. 1

Assembling the House
Use icing as "glue" on the backs of the gingerbread pieces to adhere them to other pieces, holding the pieces in place until the icing begins to harden.
1. Adhere the windows, shutters, and door to the front piece, leaving about ¹/₂" between the bottom of the house and the bottom of the door. Adhere the chimney to one side piece. Assemble the chimney top pieces.
2. Brush the windows with corn syrup and sprinkle with edible glitter; let dry. Pipe the windows, shutters, and chimney bricks. Pipe the door outlines; then, thin 3 tablespoons of icing with a little water and use the spatula to fill in the door (Fig. 1). Add a silver dragée for the doorknob.
3. Use the spatula to spread icing on the porch roof pieces; sprinkle with edible glitter before the icing dries.
4. Let all the pieces sit a few hours before assembling the house.
5. Use a cardboard box to support the inside of the gingerbread house. To build a box the size we used, cut two 14¹/₂"w x 11¹/₂"h front/back pieces and two 7¹/₂"w x 11¹/₂"h sides. Hot glue the side edges of the pieces together and glue the bottom edges to the foam core base.
6. Use icing to adhere the front gingerbread piece, then the side and back pieces to the box. Pipe icing along the side edges of the house. Let the pieces sit a few hours before adding the roof.
7. Pipe icing along the top edges of the house, adhere the roof pieces, and pipe along the roof peak. Adhere the chimney top to the roof.
8. Adhere the porch piece to the foam core base. Adhere dowels to the back of each column. Adhere the bottoms of the columns to the porch about 3" from the house. Pipe icing on the tops of the columns and door and adhere the porch roof pieces, resting them on top of the door for support. Pipe icing along the peak of the porch roof.
9. Pipe lines on the roof pieces and add dragées at the intersections. Pipe icicles around the chimney top and along the house and porch roof edges. Hot glue greenery to the base. Sprinkle artificial snow around the house.

• Royal Icing • pastry brush • light corn syrup • white edible glitter • small rubber spatula • silver dragées (nonedible; for decoration only) • cardboard box or heavy cardboard • hot glue gun • 20" x 26" piece of foam core • ¹/₈"dia. dowel cut into two 6" lengths • snow tipped greenery sprigs • artificial snow

Appliqué Stockings

(from page 59)

For a distinctive duo, stitch a brown stocking with cream appliqué and partner it with a cream stocking appliquéd in brown. Match raw edges and use a 1/2" seam allowance unless otherwise noted.

1. For each stocking, enlarge one of the floral patterns (page 151) to 183%. Transfer the pattern onto the appliqué fabric; cut out along the outer edges. Draw over the transferred flower and stem lines with the fabric pen to ensure that the lines won't rub off while sewing.

2. Enlarge the stocking pattern (page 152) to 208%. Using the pattern, cut two lining pieces (one in reverse). Draw around the pattern twice (once in reverse) on the stocking fabric; do not cut out.

3. Layer and pin the appliqué piece on one stocking piece, matching the raw edges of the appliqué with the outer edges of the stocking pattern. Using metallic thread, zigzag along the design lines to sew the pieces together. Refer to the photos to cut out the appliqué close to the stitching, being careful not to cut through the stocking fabric. Cut out the stocking pieces.

4. Matching right sides, sew the stocking front and back together along the side and bottom edges; clip the curves and turn right side out. Repeat for the lining fabric, leaving an opening along one side edge for turning; do not turn right side out. Sew beads to the flower centers on the stocking.

5. To make the cording, press one end of a 1 3/4" x 16" strip of lining fabric 1/2" to the wrong side. Beginning 1/2" from the pressed end, center a 16" cord length on the wrong side of the strip. Matching long edges, fold the strip over the cord. Using a zipper foot, sew next to the cord. Trim the flange to 1/2".

6. Beginning and ending 2" from the cording ends, baste the flange of the cording along the top of the stocking. Trimming to fit, insert the unfinished cord end into the pressed end of the cording and finish basting.

7. Place the stocking inside the lining and pin the top edges together, inserting a ribbon loop for the hanger between the stocking and the lining at the heel-side seam. Sew along the top edges. Turn right side out, sew the opening closed, and tuck the lining in the stocking.

For each stocking you will need:
• blue transfer paper • 12" x 15" piece of cotton velvet for the appliqué • water-soluble fabric pen • 1/2 yd of cotton velvet for lining and cording • 3/8 yd of cotton velvet for stocking (the color should contrast with the appliqué fabric) • metallic gold thread • small, sharp scissors • gold beads • beading needle • 7/32" dia. cotton cord • 3/8"w velveteen ribbon

Cream Silk Stockings

(from page 58)

Snow on snow—the silk stockings are crowned with velveteen cuffs and sprinkled with sparkling beads. Match raw edges and use a 1/2" seam allowance unless otherwise noted.

1. For each stocking, enlarge the patterns (page 154) to 213%. Using the pattern, cut two stocking pieces (one in reverse). Repeat for the lining fabric. Using the enlarged pattern, cut a velveteen cuff.

2. Matching right sides, sew the stocking front and back together along the side and bottom edges; clip the curves and turn right side out. Repeat for the lining; do not turn right side out. Sew beads to the stocking front where desired.

3. Place the lining inside the stocking and baste them together along the top edges. Using scraps of velveteen for pressing cloths, hem the pointed edge of the cuff with fusible tape. Matching right sides, sew the short edges together; turn right side out. Place the cuff inside the stocking, aligning the heel-side seams. Fold the ribbon in half. Matching the fold with the top of the stocking, tuck the ribbon between the stocking and the cuff at the heel-side seam. Sew the cuff to the stocking along the top edges; turn the cuff right side out and tie the ribbon into a loop.

For each stocking you will need:
• 3/8 yd of cream silk for stocking • 3/8 yd of cream cotton fabric for lining
• 1/4 yd of cream velveteen for the cuff • clear silver-lined E beads • beading needle • 1/4"w fusible web tape • 1 yd of 1 1/2"w cream wire-edged ribbon

Paperwhites Arrangement

(from page 61)

For the formal living room, what could be a more graceful centerpiece than paperwhites and black satin ribbon? In mid-November, fill the planter three-quarters full of potting soil for flowers that will bloom in time for Christmas. Place the bulbs in the planter about 1/2" apart, with the pointed end up. Add more soil, leaving the tops peeking out. Water thoroughly; then, set the planter in a cool dark place, checking from time to time to keep the soil moist. When the sprouts start growing in a week or two, move the planter to a bright spot away from direct sunlight.

When the flowers begin to bloom, place the planter inside the decorative container and cover the soil with moss. Place a trailing ribbon bow at the base of the flowers and add ornaments attached to floral picks.

• planter (a little smaller than the decorative container)
• potting soil • paperwhite narcissus bulbs • decorative container • dried moss • black ribbon • miniature ornaments • wired wooden floral picks

Fragrant Arrangement

(from page 60)

This breathtaking arrangement is as aromatic as it is lovely. Stack the bowls on the mirror. Line the large bowl with greenery and place herbs in the smaller bowl. Fill the bowls with limes and arrange the candles and ornaments on the mirror.

• large and small footed glass bowls • round mirror • fresh greenery (we used arborvitae) • fresh herbs (we used rosemary and sage) • limes • votives in glass holders (never leave burning candles unattended) • beaded and glass ornaments

Roses on the Snow

(from page 62)

Combine candlelight, rosebuds, and snowflakes for a delightful coffee table arrangement. Place the glass tabletop on the laminate, draw around the tabletop, then set it aside. Enlarge the snowflake designs (page 148) to 185% and make several copies of each. (We used three large flakes and four small ones with some small pieces running off the edge of the circle.) Cut the flakes apart; then, arrange and tape them to the paper side of the laminate circle. Cut out the snowflakes, being sure to cut out the center circles on the large flakes. Peel off the paper backing and adhere the flakes to the tabletop.

Spray paint the tabletop with three to four even coats. Let the paint dry to the touch; then, peel off the laminate pieces. Allow the paint to dry completely before placing the tabletop on the coffee table, painted side down.

Add greenery sprigs, rosebuds, and candles to the silver pieces and arrange them on the glass tabletop.

• 19¹/₄" dia. glass tabletop • clear adhesive laminate • tape • white spray paint • greenery sprigs • white rosebuds • white taper candles (never leave burning candles unattended) • silver mint julep cups and candelabra

Three French Hens 🍃
(from page 63)
Complement the greens and golds in your living room with this elegant arrangement.
1. To shape the birds, cover each ball with Paperclay, dipping your finger in water and smoothing as you go. Mold one end into a tail and the opposite end into a head. After the clay dries, spray the birds with adhesive and cover them with gold leaf. Use the needle to pierce small holes in the sides of the birds for the wings. Trim the feathers and insert the quills in the holes.
2. Apply adhesive and cover the dowels with silver leaf and the 5" plaques with a mixture of gold and silver leaf. Use the awl to pierce the bottom of each bird. Insert one end of the dowel in the bird and hot glue the other end in the center of a wheel.
3. Hot glue moss around each wheel and cone. Hot glue the bottom of each cone to a 5" plaque. To add beads to the trees, thread each bead on a 1½" wire length and insert the ends in the tree.
4. Place the saucer on the coffee table, centering the wooden base on top. Arrange the trees, birds, and ornaments on the plaque. Add greenery under the arrangement.

• three 1¾" dia. foam balls • Creative Paperclay® • gold and silver leaf with spray adhesive • large needle • white feathers • ³/₁₆" dia. dowels cut to 3", 4½", and 6" lengths • two 5" dia. wood plaques • awl • hot glue gun • three 2" dia. wooden toy wheels • dried moss • 9" and 12"h foam cones with 4½" dia. bases • round gold beads • florist's wire • wire cutters • saucer or shallow bowl • 14" dia. painted wooden base • gold and silver ornaments • fresh greenery

Welcome Mat 🍃
(from page 66)
Greet your guests with this striking holiday mat. Spray paint the doormat and let it dry. Enlarge the deer pattern (page 155) to 400% and the "Noel" patterns to 200%. Cut the patterns from template plastic and stencil the designs onto the mat with craft paint.

• red spray paint • coir doormat (ours measures 19" x 29½") • quilter's template plastic • gold and brown craft paint • stencil brushes

Hydrangea Garland
(from page 65)

For a grand entranceway, wire together greenery, berry, and silver leaf garlands in an asymmetrical design to hang over the top and one side of your front door. Add grass, berry, and hydrangea picks to the garland. Spread a little silver paste on the stars, allowing the copper to show through in places. Wire the stars to the corner. If you like, thread mini lights through the arrangement for extra shimmer.

• heavy-gauge floral wire • wire cutters • artificial mixed greenery garland • green berry garland • silver leaf garland • silvery grass picks • green berry picks • large glittered green hydrangea picks • silver wax metallic finish paste • one large and two small copper stars • mini light strand (optional)

Pine Door Spray
(from page 61)

Grace your front door with a distinctive spray that is surprisingly simple to put together. Wire branches together a few inches from the top and add in the large pinecones. Next wire the ornaments, then the medium pinecones to the greenery. Add ribbon streamers and a bow to the top of the spray.

• medium-gauge wire • wire cutters • mixed greenery branches (some of ours are snow-flocked) • oversized pinecones • gold glass ball ornaments • gold crackle ornaments • medium pinecones • gold satin ribbon

Give

The best sound in the world may be the tearing of gift wrap, because you know what's coming next—squeals of glee and exclamations of "How did you know?" Since the beginning of the gift-giving tradition, handmade presents have had that heartwarming effect. And because you put care and affection into the creation of each gift, you know they are memorable and worthy— just like the recipients.

Date Night Gift Card Set

Offer your services as a babysitter and send the new parents out for a night on the town. Instructions are on page 98.

Sometimes, the most thoughtful gift is a small plastic rectangle.

Your uncle already has everything. Your cousin just moved into a new house. You're sure your sister-in-law would love tickets to a show, but you can't guess which evening would work best for her. Gift cards make it possible for the recipient to choose a present at their convenience. If you're worried that a gift card is too impersonal, use all the time you saved on shopping and gift wrapping to create a presentation box or bag. Then there'll be no doubt that a little extra thought went into selecting the perfect gift.

Pop-Up Gift Card Holder
Put a little fun into your gift-giving!
Instructions are on page 99.

Bag of Gold
At Christmas, a gift card is every bit as good as gold. Instructions are on page 100.

Slow down just a little. The flip side of being the family decorator, shopper, present wrapper, and baker is that you may miss your chance to just inhale the scents, see the sights, and feel the quiet joy. Christmas will feel as though it's lasting longer if you simply stop and let its meaning enfold you.

The season has its own gifts to give. Don't miss yours in the holiday rush.

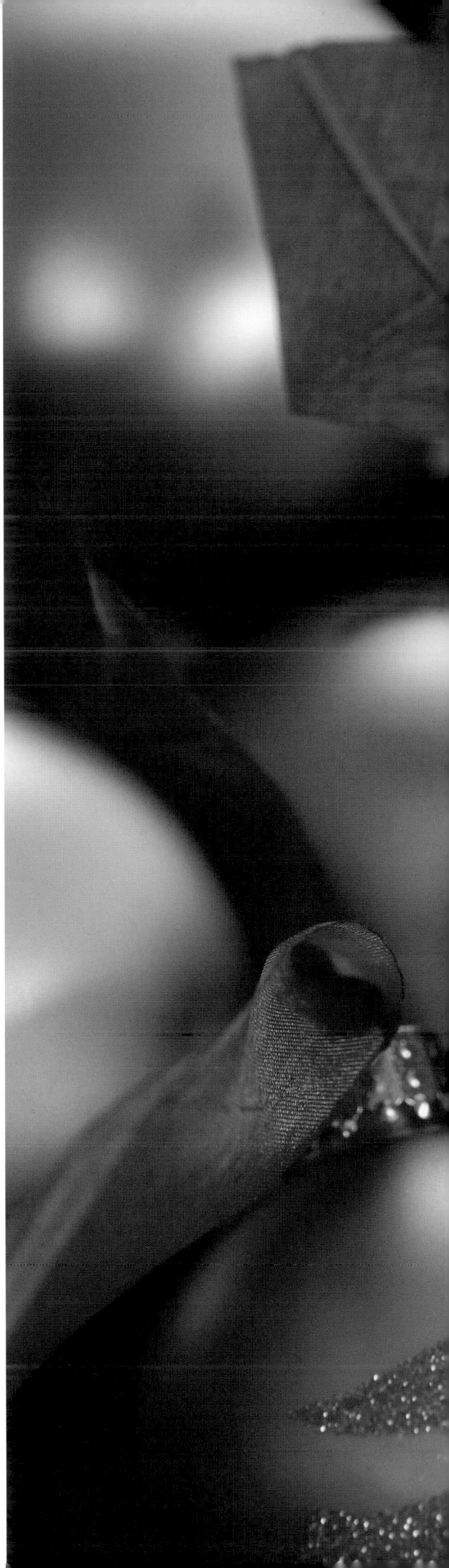

Peaceful, pretty—and completed in an instant. Each Christmas, keep a few by the front door for last-minute gifts. Instructions are on page 100.

S-s-s-snake!
The best way to let a tough
guy know he's adorable?
Give him a corduroy python
for a reading companion.
Instructions are on page 102.

They invite you to go on digs for dinosaur bones. They make you proud at dance recitals. Best of all, they're thrilled when they can bring you a gift they made with their own two hands. This year, return the favor to those amazing kids with at least one present that didn't come from Santa or the department store. A giant python or a bird-shaped purse with button eyes will capture their imaginations. While toys that light up and make noises will hold their attention for a little while, your handmade gifts will have real staying power. And once you've experienced the magic of creating kid stuff, you'll want to make it a regular part of every Christmas.

Blue Bag of Happiness
She'll take it everywhere she goes—not only because of the cool fabrics, but also because you made it. Instructions are on page 101.

Canine Cover-up
All dressed up and ready
to go. Instructions for the
coat are on page 105.

Remember...
Love the animals: God has
given them the rudiments of
thought and joy untroubled.
Fyodor Dostoyevsky

Remember the day you picked out that wiggly pup? Or the time that curious kitten found you? That fuzzy-faced charmer is a member of the family now, one who enjoys the holiday tradition of getting gifts for Christmas. Which means the pet toys have been accumulating for a while. Mittens is probably getting a little bored with all her plastic jingling toys. Laddie is trying to hide his old rawhide chews in the sofa cushions (along with a bagel the kids gave him this morning). This year, why not surprise the fur person with something new? A warm jacket, stuffed toy fish, or soft pet bed are nice creature comforts you can make for your four-legged friend. In return, you'll get the fun of seeing the world's best pet enjoy your handiwork.

Fish out of Water
Penny takes the innocent approach before reeling in a record catch. Instructions for the catnip fish are on page 103.

Center of Attention
Bingo's new comfort zone—a cozy bed where he can keep an eye on all his favorite humans. Instructions for the box-cushion bed are on page 104.

Window shopping, browsing the Internet, leafing through catalogs—matching the gift with the recipient is exciting. It's even more fun when you put the gift together yourself. If your best friend loves to cook for guests, a personalized apron is an excellent present. However, if she's a young mom who has no time for entertaining, the perfect gift may be a basket filled with family-friendly DVDs and snacks like white chocolate popcorn. Add the latest best-seller so she can enjoy a good read after the kids (finally!) fall asleep.

Giving either of these thoughtful gifts can easily become a yearly event.

Scalloped Apron
Every cook needs a fashionable apron that's theirs alone.
Instructions are on page 106.

White Chocolate Popcorn

24	cups of popped popcorn
$3/4$	cup butter or margarine
2	cups firmly packed brown sugar
$1/2$	cup light corn syrup
1	teaspoon salt
1	teaspoon vanilla extract
$1/2$	teaspoon baking soda
8	ounces white candy coating, chopped
4	ounces white baking chocolate, chopped

Place popcorn in a lightly greased large roasting pan. In a heavy large saucepan, melt butter over medium heat. Stir in brown sugar, corn syrup, and salt. Stirring constantly, bring mixture to a boil. Boil 5 minutes without stirring. Remove from heat. Stir in vanilla and baking soda (mixture will foam). Pour syrup over popcorn; stir until well coated. Bake at 250° for 1 hour, stirring every 15 minutes. Spread on lightly greased aluminum foil. In a small saucepan, melt candy coating and chocolate over low heat. Drizzle melted chocolate mixture over popcorn. Let chocolate harden (about 30 minutes). Store popcorn in an airtight container.
Yield: about 27 cups popcorn

Remember...

a gift basket doesn't have to be a basket. You can use a flowerpot, tool box, oversized tin, or any other container that will fit the theme of your gift.

Movie Night Basket
Just add family. Instructions are on page 107.

Ham Basket
A nice ham with
seasoning and sauce—the
recipient will hope this gift is
a new tradition! Instructions
are on page 108.

Ham Rub

1 cup firmly packed brown
    sugar
1 teaspoon dry mustard
1 teaspoon ground cloves
1 teaspoon ground ginger
1 teaspoon ground nutmeg

Combine all ingredients and store in a resealable plastic bag. Give with serving instructions.

To serve, spread rub over outside of ham before baking.
Yield: 1$\frac{1}{2}$ cups rub

Cranberry-Pineapple Sauce

A great sauce that can be served with a variety of meats.

1 package (12 ounces) fresh
    cranberries
1$\frac{1}{3}$ cups sugar
$\frac{3}{4}$ cup chopped red onion
$\frac{1}{3}$ cup water
$\frac{1}{3}$ cup orange juice
1 can (8 ounces) crushed
    pineapple, drained
$\frac{1}{4}$ teaspoon dried orange
    peel

Combine cranberries, sugar, onion, water, and orange juice in a saucepan over medium heat; cook until cranberries pop and mixture begins to thicken, about 7 to 10 minutes. Add pineapple and orange peel and continue cooking until heated through, stirring occasionally. Serve with cooked ham.
Yield: about 3 cups sauce

Goodness-to-Go Jars
From ordinary jar to a pretty pail of preserves. The beaded bale hints at the richness inside. Instructions are on page 108.

Pumpkin-Apple Butter

2 cans (15 ounces each) canned pumpkin
2 cups peeled, cored, and shredded Granny Smith apples
2 cups no-sugar-added apple juice
1 cup firmly packed brown sugar
2 teaspoons ground cinnamon
1 teaspoon ground ginger
$\frac{1}{2}$ teaspoon ground cloves
$\frac{1}{4}$ teaspoon salt

Combine all ingredients in a 4-quart slow cooker. Cook on HIGH for 5 hours, stirring every 2 hours. Store in a covered container in the refrigerator for up to 2 months.
Yield: about 5$\frac{1}{2}$ cups pumpkin-apple butter

Ornament Gift Tag
Once given, the gift tag can go from plate to tree.
Instructions are on page 109.

Chocolate Angel Food Cupcakes

$1/4$ cup plus 1 tablespoon baking cocoa, divided
1 package (16 ounces) angel food cake mix
$1^1/2$ teaspoons almond extract, divided
$1/2$ cup sliced almonds
$1^1/2$ cups powdered sugar, divided
2 tablespoons water, divided

Line a muffin pan with foil muffin cups. Stir $1/4$ cup of cocoa into dry cake mix. Prepare cake mix according to package directions, adding 1 teaspoon almond extract. Fill muffin cups about two-thirds full. Sprinkle almonds over batter. Bake at 350° for 18 to 20 minutes or until tops are lightly brown. Cool in pan on a wire rack. Transfer cupcakes to a wire rack with waxed paper underneath.

For the white glaze, combine $3/4$ cup powdered sugar, $1/4$ teaspoon almond extract, and 1 tablespoon water in a small bowl; drizzle over half of the cupcakes. For the chocolate glaze, combine $3/4$ cup powdered sugar, 1 tablespoon cocoa, $1/4$ teaspoon almond extract, and remaining 1 tablespoon water in a small bowl; drizzle over remaining cupcakes. Allow glazes to harden. Store in an airtight container.
Yield: about $2^1/2$ dozen cupcakes

Garlic-Flavored Pita Chips

5 pita breads, halved and split
$2/3$ cup olive oil
$1^1/2$ teaspoons garlic powder
$3/4$ teaspoon ground cumin
2 tablespoons dried parsley flakes

Cut each pita bread piece into 4 wedges. Place wedges on ungreased baking sheets. Combine oil, garlic powder, cumin, and parsley in a small bowl. Brush each wedge with oil mixture. Bake at 400° for 8 to 10 minutes or until lightly browned and crispy.
Yield: 80 pita chips

Roasted Red Pepper Hummus

This is especially good served on Garlic-Flavored Pita Chips.

- 2 cans (15 ounces each) chickpeas
- 1 jar (7 ounces) whole roasted red peppers in olive oil
- 6 tablespoons lemon juice
- 1/4 cup tahini (sesame seed paste)
- 2 garlic cloves, minced
- 3/4 teaspoon salt
- 3/4 teaspoon ground cumin
- 1/2 teaspoon ground cayenne pepper

Purée all ingredients in a food processor until mixture is smooth, scraping the sides of the container several times. Store in an airtight container in the refrigerator for at least 1 hour to allow flavors to blend. (Hummus will keep in the refrigerator for 3 days.) Serve at room temperature.

Yield: about 4 cups hummus

Remember...

It's not how much we give
but how much love we
put into giving.

Mother Teresa of Calcutta

Hummus and Pita Bowl
A zesty snack, with serving bowls thoughtfully included. Instructions are on page 109.

Here's How

Date Night
Gift Card Set
(from pages 82 and 84)

Great to give to new parents, newlyweds, or your significant other.

1. Paint the box inside and out and allow to dry. Use spray adhesive to adhere scrapbook paper pieces to the top, sides, and inner compartments of the box.

2. Apply a few coats of varnish, allowing the box to dry between coats.

3. Write "dinner," "movie," "dessert," and "enjoy" on the tags. Rub "Date Night" on the first compartment. Glue ribbon lengths across the other three compartments and add a tag to each. Slip a gift card under each ribbon.

4. Tie ribbon around the box and attach the "enjoy" tag to the bow.

- acrylic paint
- paintbrushes
- wooden box with four compartments (our box is 4³/₈"w x 6"l x 1¹/₄"h)
- spray adhesive
- scrapbook paper • clear acrylic matte varnish • fine-point permanent marker
- four round metal tags
- alphabet rub-ons • craft glue • ³/₈"w velvet ribbon
- gift cards • ¹/₈" dia. hole punch • embroidery floss

Pop-Up Gift Card Holder
(from page 85)

Pull the ribbon down and watch the smiles pop up, along with a gift card! Use a $1/4$" seam allowance for all sewing.

1. Iron stabilizer to the back of the silk fabric pieces. Use the pattern (page 154) and cut two holly leaves from green fabric; set aside. Cut two $3^3/4$" x $4^3/4$" red pieces. Press one short end of each piece $1/4$" to the wrong side twice.

2. Topstitch the pressed end of one piece. Pierce a small hole $1^1/2$" below the center of the finished end; set the grommet over the hole.

3. Match wrong sides and follow Fig. 1 to pin one end of an 8" ribbon length under the pressed end of the remaining fabric piece; topstitch the pressed end.

4. Matching right sides, sew the pieces together along the side and bottom edges, being careful not to catch the ribbon in the stitching. Turn right side out and topstitch along the seams. Pull the ribbon end through the grommet. Place the gift card in the holder (this will draw up the ribbon). Trimming the ribbon as desired, sew the tag to the ribbon end. Write "Pull" on the tag.

5. Sew the bells and leaves to the front of the card holder. Glue two 9" ribbon lengths back-to-back and glue the ends to the back of the holder for the handle.

Fig. 1

• fabric stabilizer • green silk fabric scrap • $1/8$ yd red silk fabric • tracing paper • awl or craft knife • brass grommet with $1/4$" dia. opening and setter • hammer • $3/8$"w green velvet ribbon • gift card • $5/8$" square metal tag • fine-point permanent marker • three mini jingle bells • fabric glue

Bag of Gold 🍃
(from page 85)

This quick-to-make pouch will add personality to the gift card tucked inside. Match right sides and use a 1/4" seam allowance for all sewing.

1. Cut a 5" x 12 1/2" piece each from the bag and lining fabrics. Matching short ends, sew the bag sides together; turn right side out. Matching short ends and leaving an opening for turning, sew the lining sides together; do not turn right side out.

2. Place the bag inside the lining. Fold the ribbon in half and tuck it between the bag and the lining, pinning the fold to the center top of the bag. Sew the bag and lining together along the top edges. Turn right side out and sew the opening closed. Tuck the lining inside the bag.

3. Place the gift card inside the bag and wrap it up with the ribbon ties. Write a message on a pinked muslin tag. Sew the appliqué and tag to the pouch.

- 1/4 yd bag fabric • 1/4 yd lining fabric
- 3/4 yd of 1/4"w ribbon • gift card
- fabric marker • pinking shears
- muslin scrap • sequin appliqué

Turtledove Ornaments 🍃
(from page 87)

So easy to do, you'll want to make them for all of your friends. For each ornament, trace the pattern (page 149) onto an adhesive sheet. Cut out the dove and peel the backing from one side. Adhere the dove to the ornament, smoothing down all the edges. Peel off the remaining backing. Holding the ornament over a paper plate, sprinkle glitter on the adhesive and shake off the excess. Tie ribbon to the hanger.

- double-sided adhesive sheet • glass ornament
- paper plate • fine glitter • 1 1/2"w crinkled ribbon

Blue Bag of Happiness

(from page 89)

That young girl on your list will love this sweet purse. Use a $1/4$" seam allowance for all sewing.

1. Fuse web to the wrong side of the bird back and wing fabrics. Enlarge the patterns (page 152), to 200%. Using the patterns, fold each fabric in half and cut two backs and two wings (one of each will be in reverse). Fold the body and lining fabrics in half and cut two bird bodies from each (one of each will be in reverse). *Note:* the bird body pattern is the entire bird shape. The back and wing will be fused on top of the body piece.

2. Using the enlarged patterns, cut one beak and two feet from gold felt. Cut two $1 1/8$" dia. circles from white felt for the eyes.

3. Remove the paper backing and fuse one back and one wing to each body. Pin the eyes in place. Zigzag along the edges of each wing, back, and eye. Fold the beak in half (as marked on the pattern) and with the fold at the top, pin the beak to one body piece (Fig. 1).

4. Matching right sides, sew the body pieces together along the underside between A and B (the top of the bird between the handles is the purse opening); clip the curves and turn right side out. Leaving an opening along the belly for turning, repeat to sew the lining pieces together; do not turn right side out.

5. Place the body inside the lining. Sew the pieces together along the top edges; turn the purse right side out and sew the opening in the lining closed. Tuck the lining inside the purse.

6. Cut a $2 1/2$" x 39" piece of strap fabric. Press one long edge $1/2$" to the wrong side. Press the opposite edge $1/4$", then $3/4$" to the wrong side and zigzag in place.

7. Pinch the strap ends lengthwise and pin them between the purse front and back at the head and tail. Zigzag in place.

8. Cut a $1 1/2$" x 6" piece of lining fabric for the legs. Press one long edge $1/2$" to the wrong side. Press the opposite edge $1/4$" to the wrong side twice and zigzag in place. Cut the piece in two and sew a foot on one end of each leg. Sew a $3/4$" button and a leg to each side of the purse. Sew a $7/8$" button to the center of each eye.

• paper-backed fusible web • $1/4$ yd each of bird body, back, and purse lining fabrics • fabric scrap for wings
• gold and white felt scraps • $1/8$ yd fabric for strap
• two $3/4$" and two $7/8$" dia. buttons

Fig. 1

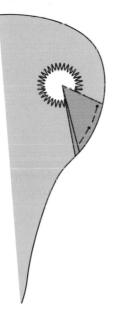

S-s-s-snake! 🐍

(from page 88)

What boy (or girl) wouldn't love to curl up with a cozy corduroy snake? Use a $1/2$" seam allowance for all sewing.

1. Enlarge the patterns (page 153) as desired (see Sizing Patterns, page 158; we copied ours at 200%). Trace the lines shown in blue on the pattern onto tracing paper for the underside snake head and tail patterns and those shown in red for the topside patterns; cut apart.

Note: The underside is narrower than the topside so the body will be flat on bottom and rounded on top.

2. To make the underside and topside body patterns, cut two kraft paper pieces the desired length of the snake and tape the head and tail patterns in place. Draw lines connecting the head and tail patterns. Cut the snake underside and topside from corduroy.

3. Sew the pleat where shown on the topside head only. Use metallic thread to zigzag corduroy scrap spots to the snake topside (we used 2" dia. spots).

4. Sew a Running Stitch (page 158) along the topside tail as shown by dashed lines on the pattern. Matching right sides and gathering the topside tail to fit, pin the snake topside and underside together.

5. Leaving an 18" opening along the middle of one side, sew the topside and underside together. Clip the curves and turn right side out. Stuff the head, then the tail and body of the snake loosely enough to keep the snake pliable. Sew the opening closed.

6. To add the eyes, double a 36" length of heavy-duty thread on the doll needle. Sew one button in place; then, run the needle under the fabric and through the remaining button. Pulling the thread taut to tuft the fabric, sew on the button.

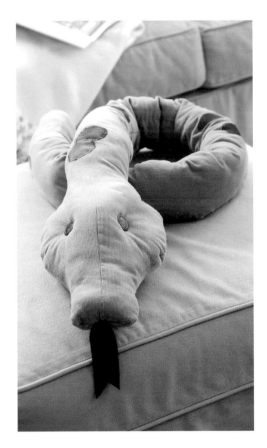

• tracing paper • kraft paper • tape • corduroy fabric (we used $1^3/_4$ yds for a 60" long snake)
• bronze metallic sewing machine thread • corduroy scraps for spots • polyester fiberfill
• heavy-duty thread • doll needle • two $3/_4$" dia. shank-style buttons • felt scrap for tongue

Fish out of Water

(from page 91)

Arouse your favorite Kitty's curiosity with this splashy fish. Match right sides and use a $1/4$" seam allowance for all sewing.

1. Fold the fish and dotted fabric pieces in half. Enlarge the patterns (page 150) to 160% and cut one fish and three fins from the doubled fabrics. Cut a gusset from a single layer of dotted fabric. Use the fabric pen to lightly mark the fin placement on the right sides of the fish pieces, and A and B on the wrong side of one fish piece.

2. Leaving the straight ends open, sew each fin pair together; clip the curves, turn right side out, and press. Matching raw edges, pin, then baste a fin to the top and bottom of one fish piece where marked. Pin, then baste the remaining fin to the bottom of the remaining fish piece.

3. Leaving the belly edge open, sew the fish pieces together between A and B. Clip the curves. Leaving an opening for turning, sew the gusset to the belly of the fish; clip the curves and turn right side out. Stuff the fish and sew the opening closed.

4. For each eye, cut a $1/2$" dia. felt circle and attach each to the fish with a French knot (page 158).

5. Spray the fish with catnip spray, refreshing as needed.

• $1/8$ yd fabric for fish • $1/8$ yd dotted fabric for fins and gusset • water-soluble fabric pen • polyester fiberfill • felt scrap for eyes • embroidery floss • catnip spray

Center of Attention

(from page 91)

We made a 24" square pillow for our dog. Adjust the size of the pillow form, fabrics, and patterns (see Sizing Patterns, page 158) to fit your pooch. Match right sides and use a ¹/₂" seam allowance for all sewing.

1. Cut two 25" squares from pillow fabric and two 5" x 52" corduroy strips. Sew the strips together along one end and press the seam open to make the boxing strip.

2. Enlarge the patterns (page 152) to 165%. Trace them onto fusible web, repeating as desired to make 16 dogs (or use free downloads printed from the internet showing your dog's breed in different poses). Cut the patterns apart as needed and fuse the web to the black fabric; cut out the silhouettes (the silhouettes will be the reverse of the patterns). Remove the paper backing.

3. To mark silhouette placement, align one end of the boxing strip with one edge of the pillow top. Center and pin four silhouettes on the strip, leaving 1"–2" where the strip will wrap around the corners (Fig. 1). Continue to space and pin the remaining silhouettes (there will be a little extra fabric at the end of the strip).

4. Fuse the silhouettes in place; then, use nylon thread and zigzag around the edges.

5. Pin and baste cording around the pillow top and bottom. Clip the corners.

6. Matching raw edges, pin the boxing strip to the pillow top. Trim the ends of the strip to overlap ¹/₂".

7. Beginning ¹/₂" from one end of the strip, sew the strip to the pillow top. Sew the ends of the strip together. Leaving one side open for stuffing, sew the strip to the pillow bottom. Clip the corners, turn right side out, and insert the pillow form. Stuff the corners with fiberfill. Sew the opening closed.

8. Cover the buttons with corduroy and use heavy-duty thread and the upholstery needle to sew one button to the center back of the pillow. Insert the needle through the pillow and the remaining button. Take the needle back through the pillow and the back button, pulling tightly to tuft. Repeat as desired, each time knotting the thread ends at the back.

Fig. 1

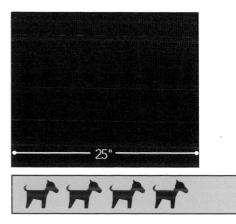

25"

• ³/₄ yd of 54"w upholstery fabric for pillow top and bottom • ¹/₄ yd of 54"w light-colored corduroy for boxing strip • ¹/₂ yd of 18"w paper-backed fusible web • ¹/₄ yd black cotton fabric • smoke colored nylon thread • 5³/₄ yds decorative cording with flange • 24" x 24" x 4" boxed pillow form • polyester fiberfill • two 2¹/₂" self-cover buttons • heavy-duty thread • upholstery needle

Canine Cover-up
(from page 90)

With only two measurements you'll soon tailor-make this sophisticated cape to fit your favorite Fifi. Match right sides and use a 1/4" seam allowance for all sewing.

1. To size the patterns to fit your dog, measure around the dog's chest behind the front legs and add 3". Divide this number by 11. Multiply the result by 100. Photocopy the coat and collar half patterns at this percentage.

2. To be sure the neckline of the sized pattern will fit your dog (since dog proportions vary), measure around your dog's neck and divide by 2. Measure the half pattern neckline from the pleat stitching line to the end of the neck tab. Make sure this is at least 1 1/2" larger than the half neck measurement. Adjust the neckline tab and collar pattern if needed to fit your dog.

3. Matching right sides, fold the wool fabric in half. Align the pattern fold line with the fold of the fabric and cut one wool coat piece; do not unfold. Use pins to mark the pleat stitching line and dot. Sew from the neckline to the dot through both fabric thicknesses. Unfold the coat and press the box pleat (Fig. 1). Repeat for the coat lining piece.

4. Using the collar half pattern, cut a collar each from folded lining fabric and faux fur; unfold. Leaving the inside curve open, sew the collar pieces together. Clip curves and turn right side out.

5. Center and pin the collar (right side up) to the coat neckline (right side up); baste. Sew buttons to the coat at the top of the pleat. Leaving an opening at the end of one neck tab, sew the coat and lining together. Clip corners and curves and turn right side out. Sew the opening closed and press.

6. Topstitch along the coat edges. Sew hook-and-loop fasteners to the neck and tummy tabs.

• wool suiting fabric • suit lining fabric • faux fur • two 1/2" dia. black shank buttons • two 3/4"w hook- and-loop fastener strips

Fig. 1

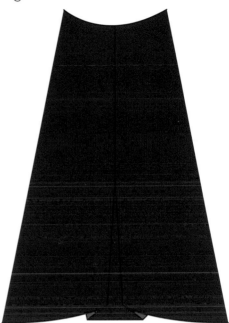

Pleat

• ⅞ yd print fabric • ⅞ yd lining fabric • ¼ yd pocket fabric • 4"h iron-on monogram • 3½ yds of 1¼"w twill tape • safety pins • water-soluble fabric pen • three 1½" D-rings

Scalloped Apron

(from page 92)

Thrill someone who loves to cook with her own monogrammed apron. For a more tailored version, omit the scalloped hem. Use a ¼" seam allowance for all sewing unless otherwise noted.

1. Enlarge each pattern (page 156) to 204%; cut out.

2. Matching right sides and long edges, fold a 28½" x 38" print fabric piece in half. Aligning the straight edges of the pattern with the fabric edges, pin the armhole pattern on the top corner of the fabric opposite the fold. Cutting through all thicknesses, cut away the armholes. Repeat to cut the lining piece.

3. Using the pattern, cut a pocket from pocket fabric. Zigzag along the top edge. Press the edges ½" to the wrong side, clipping curves as needed. Pin the pocket to the apron front about 6" from the side and 12" from the bottom (Fig. 1). Topstitch the pocket to the apron. Iron the monogram on the pocket.

4. For each tie, baste one end of a 40" twill tape length to the right side of the apron ½" below the bottom of each armhole. Pin the loose tie ends to the middle of the apron (Fig. 2).

5. Matching right sides, pin the lining to the apron. Aligning the long straight edge of the pattern with the bottom of the lining, use the fabric pen to draw scallops on the lining, moving the pattern as needed to complete five scallops. Leaving the top edge open, sew the lining to the apron along the armholes, sides, and on the drawn scallop lines. Cut away the excess fabric ¼" below the scallops. Clip the corners and curves and turn right side out; press.

6. Press the top edge of the apron ½", then 3½" to the back and sew along the pressed edge (this will help keep the top edge of the apron from gapping). For each neckline tab, press the ends of a 5" twill tape length ½" to the wrong side. Fold each tab in half and thread one D-ring on one tab and two D-rings on the other tab. Sew the tabs to the back of the apron (Fig. 3).

7. Topstitch along all edges of the apron. For the neck strap, press one end of a 34" twill tape length ½" to the wrong side. Thread the pressed end through the single D-ring and sew as shown (Fig. 4).

8. Trimming to fit, hem the ties and neck strap.

Fig. 1

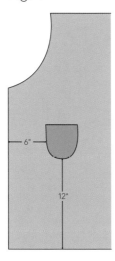

Fig. 2

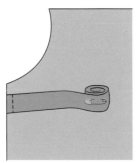

Fig. 3

Fig. 4

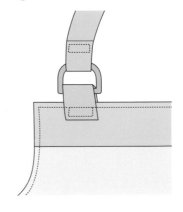

Movie Night Basket

(from page 93)

Put together a lined basket chock-full of all the ingredients for a fun and festive family night.

1. Make a paper pattern for the basket liner. Cut one paper strip the width of the basket (plus 1" for seam allowances) and line the basket with the strip, allowing 4" to drape to the outside on each end. Repeat with a strip cut the length of the basket (plus 1"). Tape the pieces together in the shape of a plus sign and use the pattern to cut the fabric.

2. Place the fabric in the basket right side out. Matching right sides, pin the corner edges together to fit the basket. Turn the liner wrong side out, sew the edges, and place the liner in the basket (wrong side out).

3. To pin a narrow rectangle marking the placement for each handle opening, follow Fig. 1 to pin along the top of the rim between the handle ends and at the outer edges of the handle. Measure the thickness of the handle and complete the top edge of the rectangle, pinning this distance above the rim.

4. Cut a wide X from corner to corner of each pinned handle area. Remove the pins and press the fabric edges to the wrong side of the liner. Topstitch along the pressed edges.

5. Press the 2"w ribbon in half, matching wrong sides and long edges. Sandwich and pin the raw liner edge between the long ribbon edges, overlapping the ends and turning the top end under. Use clear thread to zigzag the ribbon to the liner. Place the liner in the basket.

6. Fill the basket with paper shreds, bowls, popcorn, movies, and wrapped candies, along with greenery sprigs here and there. Add a special ornament to evoke movie night memories in the years ahead.

- large basket with side handles (ours is 12"w x 18"l x 7"h) • kraft paper or newsprint • tape • fabric for liner (we used 1¼ yds) • 2"w satin ribbon (we used 1¾ yds) • clear nylon thread • paper shreds • large wooden bowl with individual serving bowls for popcorn • bag of White Chocolate Popcorn in a ribbon-tied box • Christmas movies • movie-size boxed candies wrapped in scrapbook papers • greenery sprigs • ornament with long ribbon hanger

Fig. 1

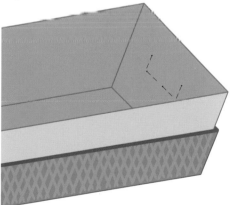

Goodness-to-Go Jars

(from page 95)

For old-fashioned flavor with an updated look, add painted lids and beaded handles to small jars of Pumpkin-Apple Butter. Prime, then paint each lid and let it dry. Fill each jar and secure the lid. Leaving a 2"-long tail, wrap medium-gauge wire around the jar just below the lid. Twist the wire around the tail; then, form a handle loop by attaching the wire to the opposite side. Curl the wire ends. String beads on fine-gauge wire and wrap it around and around the handle. Tape a scrapbook paper circle to the lid and a computer-printed cardstock label to the front of the jar.

• wide-mouthed jelly jars • metal spray primer • black metallic spray paint • Pumpkin-Apple Butter • medium- and fine-gauge wire • wire cutters • glass beads • double-stick tape • scrapbook paper • cardstock

Ham Basket

(from page 94)

This thoughtful gift begins with a sturdy wood excelsior-lined basket. Keep the ham and sauce refrigerated until just before delivery; then, place the gift-wrapped smoked ham in the basket. Add a tea towel-wrapped bottle of wine tucked in an ice bucket. To complete the entrée, include containers of Cranberry-Pineapple Sauce and Ham Rub. Fill in with greenery and berry picks and a few pinecones.

Hummus and Pita Bowl
(from page 97)
A welcome departure from customary holiday fare, this bowl of hummus and pita chips is sure to be a hit. For a festive look, add a ribbon-and-paper topper to the bag of chips and a tag to the jar of hummus. Fill the large bowl with excelsior; then, nestle a sparkly ornament in the bowl along with the snacks and ribbon-tied dipping bowl.

• ribbon • cardstock • scrapbook paper • Garlic-Flavored Pita Chips in a cellophane bag • jar of Roasted Red Pepper Hummus (keep refrigerated) • large and small bowl • wood excelsior • ornament

Ornament Gift Tag
(from page 96)
For the ornament tag, enlarge the pattern (page 156) to 150% and cut one tag each from cardstock and from cardstock-backed fabric (use spray adhesive to adhere cardstock to the back of the fabric). Glue metallic trims around the fabric edges and tape the ornament hanger to the back. Write a message on the bottom edge of the cardstock shape and, notching the top to fit around the hanger as needed, glue the shape to the back of the tag. Thread ribbon through the hanger. Wrap the plate of cupcakes with cellophane and tie it up with the ornament tag.

• cardstock • 4" square fabric piece • spray adhesive • fabric glue • metallic trims • clear tape • mini ornament with cord hanger • fine-point permanent marker • sheer metallic ribbon • plate of Chocolate Angel Food Cupcakes • cellophane

Celebrate

Is there anything more fun than spreading a table with beautiful foods? For any event you find yourself hosting at Christmastime, there are dishes that not only fit the gathering, but are destined to become new traditions. Throw a casual gift-wrapping party for a few of your closest friends. Plan time alone with someone even closer. Pull out the stops to host a formal open house with desserts and coffee, and gather with your family for memorable meals.

Tags by the Dozen
Colorful gift tags for perfect packages. See Supply Scape instructions on page 142.

There's an old saying, "Many hands make light work." And it's true—especially when it comes to the pleasant work of wrapping Christmas presents. Ask your friends to bring the gifts they need to wrap so everyone can enjoy a lively party while paper, ribbon, and laughter are shared all around. Finger foods, sweet and spicy beverages, and upbeat music keep the atmosphere charged with creativity. This kind of get-together is so much fun, it's sure to become a new tradition.

Wrapping Kits
Scissors, tape, and more—give each guest a box of gift-wrapping supplies. Instructions are on page 144.

Get the gift wrappers into a holiday frame of mind with quick and colorful decorations—heap ornaments into glass containers and organize supplies to extend the colorful display. Here's an idea to help everyone remember party highlights for next year's event: Put snapshots of everyone's packages (including any off-the-wall creations that were made just for laughs) into an album. Through the year, add magazine clippings of new gift-wrapping tips and photos.

Supply Scape and
Ribbon Holders
Instructions are
on page 142.

Wrapping Ideas
Pretty packages, each so simple to create. Instructions are on page 143.

Begin a *New* Tradition

I love Christmas. I love the tree and decorations, shopping and exchanging gifts, and singing Christmas carols. But one of my favorite things about the Christmas season is that there are so many opportunities for us to be together as a family. That's especially important now that my children are all older and it's become harder for us to get together through the year.

For the last several years, we've chosen an evening between Thanksgiving and Christmas to spend some time together without gifts, ornate dinner menus, or fancy clothes. Before everyone gets all get caught up in the frenzy of the season, we sit down together to watch a favorite Christmas movie—and the more times everyone has seen it, the better. We order pizza or have snacks and say our favorite lines, right along with the movie.

Ordinarily, we enjoy our movie night without any of the usual holiday fanfare. But last year, right before the credits rolled, my son and his wife presented each member of the family with a special Christmas gift—a little something to add to our annual movie night tradition.

Beginning this year, we'll all be watching the movie wearing our new "Shelby Family Christmas" shirts.

Rhonda Shelby
Conway, Arkansas

when planning your gift-wrapping
party, you'll need to set up a table for
food and beverages that's separate
from the worktable. It may also
be a good idea to place your party
decorations on the food table and
leave the worktable free for those
big rolls of gift wrap and other
papercrafting supplies.

All-Wrapped-Up Cookies

1/2 cup butter, softened
1/2 cup firmly packed brown sugar
3/4 cup honey
 1   egg
 1   teaspoon vanilla extract
 3   cups all-purpose flour
3/4 teaspoon baking soda
1/2 teaspoon ground cinnamon
1/4 teaspoon salt
     Red and green decorating
       sugar crystals
     Purchased red and green
       tube icing (with separate
       decorating tips)

Beat butter and brown sugar until
fluffy. Add honey, egg, and vanilla;
beat until smooth. In a separate
bowl, combine next four ingredients.
Gradually add dry ingredients to
creamed mixture; stir until a soft
dough forms. Divide dough in half.
Wrap in plastic wrap and chill
4 hours.

On a lightly floured surface, roll
out half of dough to a 10-inch square.
Cut into 2-inch squares. Sprinkle
with red decorating sugar. Transfer
to greased baking sheets. Repeat
with remaining dough, sprinkling
wih green decorating sugar. Bake
at 350° for 6 to 8 minutes. Transfer
to wire racks to cool completely.
Use a small round decorating tip on
each icing tube to pipe ribbons and
bows on cookies. Store in an airtight
container.
Yield: about 4 dozen cookies

Margarita Punch

1 liter margarita mix
1 container (6-ounce) frozen orange juice
   concentrate, thawed
   Tequila (optional)
2 liters lemon-lime soda
   Lime
   Margarita salt

Combine margarita mix, orange juice, and desired amount of tequila, if using. Stir in lemon-lime soda just before serving. Rub rims of glasses with lime and then dip in salt. Add punch.
Yield: about 13 cups punch (without tequila)

Snack Mix

6 tablespoons butter, melted
1 package (8 ounce) Italian
   salad dressing mix
2 teaspoons Worcestershire
   sauce
1/8 teaspoon garlic powder
1/8 teaspoon hot sauce
2 cups rice cereal
2 cups cheese snack crackers
2 cups pretzel sticks
2 cups bagel chips
1 cup mixed salted nuts

In a large microwave-safe bowl, combine butter, dressing mix, Worcestershire sauce, garlic powder, and hot sauce. Add cereal, crackers, pretzel sticks, bagel chips, and nuts, stirring to evenly coat. Microwave on MEDIUM for 4 to 6 minutes or until mixture is heated through, stirring after 3 minutes. Spread mixture on aluminum foil to cool; store in an airtight container.
Yield: 9 1/2 cups mix

Ham Bites

Make ahead and freeze.

4 tablespoons butter, melted
2 tablespoons mustard
1 tablespoon Worcestershire
   sauce
3/4 cup minced red onion
1 package of one dozen dinner
   rolls (the type that are
   baked together)
9 ounces thinly sliced ham
6 slices Cheddar cheese

Mix butter, mustard, Worcestershire sauce, and onion in a small bowl. Slice the entire package of rolls in half horizontally. Spread butter mixture on bottom half of rolls. Layer ham and cheese on butter mixture; replace top of rolls. Wrap in aluminum foil (can be frozen at this time) and place on a baking sheet. Bake at 350° for 12 to 15 minutes or until cheese begins to melt. Cut into 24 small sandwiches and serve warm.
Yield: 24 small sandwiches

"Warm-Your-Toes" Apple Cider

12 whole cloves
6 whole allspice
3 cinnamon sticks, broken
   in pieces
2 quarts apple cider
1 cup orange juice
1 cup cranberry juice
   cocktail
1 cup pineapple juice
1/2 cup rum
1/2 cup apple-flavored
   brandy

Place cloves, allspice, and cinnamon sticks in a 5-inch square of cheesecloth; tie with kitchen string. Pour apple cider in a large Dutch oven; add spice bag. Bring to a boil; reduce heat and cook about 35 minutes or until mixture is reduced to 4 cups. Remove spice bag and discard. Stir in remaining ingredients and cook until mixture is hot.
Yield: 8 cups cider

*I*t's the date you look forward to most during the Christmas season—the one evening the two of you always set aside for yourselves. The kids are at Grandma's. The answering machine is set to take all your calls. That's why you want the setting and the meal to be wonderful and simple to prepare. We're including some recipes that only look like you cooked all day. Just add a little more candlelight to your holiday décor, and leave only two chairs at the table. This evening is all about you two—just the way it was your first Christmas together.

Mantel Decoration
A light compote.
Instructions are on page 145.

Dinner for Two Centerpiece
Instructions are on page 144.

Pear-Feta Salad with Toasted Walnut Dressing

Pear-Feta Salad with Toasted Walnut Dressing
Salad and dressing may be prepared ahead of time and refrigerated; pour dressing on salad immediately before serving.

Pear-Feta Salad
- 2 cups mixed salad greens
- 1/4 small red onion, thinly sliced
- 1 red pear, quartered, cored, and thinly sliced (dip pears in a mixture of 3 tablespoons each water and lemon juice)

Toasted Walnut Dressing
- 1/2 cup coarsely chopped walnuts
- 1/4 cup olive oil
- 3 tablespoons red wine vinegar
- 1/2 teaspoon sugar
- 1/4 teaspoon salt
- 1/8 teaspoon white pepper
- 2 ounces feta cheese, crumbled

For salad, arrange salad greens, onion, and pear slices on 2 salad plates. Cover and refrigerate until ready to serve.

For dressing, toast walnuts in oil over medium heat in a heavy skillet about 5 minutes or until light brown. Reserving oil in skillet, place walnuts on a paper towel to drain. Add vinegar, sugar, salt, and white pepper to oil in skillet; stir over medium heat until well blended. Spoon dressing over salads and sprinkle with walnuts and cheese.
Yield: 2 servings

Roasted Asparagus
- 1/2 pound fresh asparagus
- 1 tablespoon olive oil
- 1 tablespoon butter, melted
- 1/2 teaspoon salt
- 1/4 teaspoon black pepper
- 2 teaspoons sesame seeds, toasted
- Shredded Parmesan cheese

Break off woody ends of asparagus spears; wash and drain spears. Arrange in a single layer in a baking pan. Drizzle olive oil and butter over asparagus; sprinkle salt and pepper over top. Bake at 400° for 15 minutes or until tender, but still firm to the bite. Sprinkle sesame seeds and cheese over asparagus before serving.
Yield: 2 servings

Piped Rosette Potatoes
Potatoes can be piped and chilled 3 hours ahead of time. Bring to room temperature before baking.

- 3/4 pound Yukon gold potatoes
- 2 tablespoons whipping cream
- 1 tablespoon butter, softened
- 1/2 teaspoon salt
- 1/8 teaspoon black pepper
- 1 egg yolk
- 2 tablespoons butter, melted
- 1 tablespoon dried parsley

In a medium saucepan, cover potatoes with water and cook 15 minutes or until very tender; drain and transfer potatoes to a medium bowl. Add cream, butter, salt, and pepper; blend with an electric mixer until smooth. Cool mixture 10 minutes; add egg yolk.

Transfer potato mixture into a large decorating bag, fitted with a large star tip. Pipe 3-inch rosettes onto a lightly greased baking sheet. Drizzle with melted butter and sprinkle with parsley. Bake at 400° for 15 to 17 minutes or until lightly browned around edges. Serve immediately.
Yield: five 3-inch rosettes

Beef Filets with Sautéed Mushrooms

Marinate filets 2 hours or overnight.

Marinade
- 1 cup dry red wine
- 1/4 cup chopped onion
- 2 tablespoons Worcestershire sauce
- 2 tablespoons lemon juice
- 1 garlic clove, finely minced
- 1 teaspoon ground black pepper
- 1/2 teaspoon salt
- 1 bay leaf
- 2 bacon-wrapped beef filets (6 ounces each)
- 1/4 cup butter (optional)

In a medium saucepan, combine wine and next 7 ingredients. Bring to a simmer over low heat and cook for 2 minutes; cool. Marinate filets, covered and refrigerated, at least 2 hours or overnight.

(Note: Use an instant-read thermometer to test for doneness. Cook to 145° for medium-rare, 160° for medium, and 170° for well-done.)

To cook filets in oven, heat 1/4 cup butter in a medium skillet and brown filets well on both sides. Transfer filets to a shallow roasting pan and bake at 375° until desired doneness. To grill filets, prepare a medium-hot fire. Turn filets once during cooking time and grill until desired doneness.

Sautéed Mushrooms
- 1 package (8 ounces) sliced fresh mushrooms
- 2 tablespoons butter
- 1 teaspoon Worcestershire sauce

In a medium skillet, combine all ingredients and sauté mushrooms over medium-low heat 5 minutes or until tender. Serve over beef filets.

Yield: 2 beef filets with about 1/2 cup mushrooms per filet

Chocolate Lovers' Delight

Chocolate
- 2 eggs
- 1 cup sugar
- 1/2 cup all-purpose flour
- 1/4 teaspoon salt
- 1/2 cup butter, melted
- 1/4 cup chopped pecans
- 3 tablespoons baking cocoa
- 1 teaspoon vanilla extract
  Sweetened Whipped Cream (recipe follows)

In a medium bowl, beat eggs, sugar, flour, and salt together. Stir in butter, pecans, cocoa, and vanilla. Pour mixture into a greased 9 x 5-inch loaf pan or four 4-ounce ramekins. Place in a 9 x 13-inch pan and fill pan with hot water to come halfway up sides of container(s). Bake at 300° for 40 to 50 minutes or until set. Serve warm or at room temperature with Sweetened Whipped Cream.

Yield: four 1/2-cup servings

Sweetened Whipped Cream
- 1 cup whipping cream
- 1/2 cup sugar
- 1 1/2 teaspoons vanilla extract

In a large bowl, combine all ingredients; beat at high speed until peaks form.

Yield: 2 cups

Remember . . .

serve the meal on warmed plates so you'll have more time to linger over your dinner. If you don't have a warming drawer in your kitchen, a cool oven will work for oven-safe dishes, or you can place them in hot water for a few minutes.

A mixture of artificial greenery
and painted glassware will give
you a head start on party décor.
Instructions are on page 147.

Whether it's a Christmas Day open house or your turn to host the supper club's holiday get-together—this year, enjoy the party along with your guests. Eliminate the usual stress by preparing dishes ahead of time. Your guests will be delighted by a coffee bar fully stocked with syrups and toppings—the perfect accompaniment for a wide selection of desserts. Since December evenings fill up quickly on everyone's calendar, you may be able to accommodate more of your friends by planning your event for a weekend afternoon.

Invitation
That excellent combination—elegant and easy. Instructions are on page 145.

Chocolate Caramel Brownies

1 package (11 ounces) caramel bits or a 14-ounce package of caramels
$^1/_2$ cup evaporated milk, divided
1 package (18.25 ounces) chocolate cake mix
$^3/_4$ cup butter, melted
1 teaspoon vanilla extract
1 cup walnuts, chopped

Remember...

instead of everyday wine glass charms, tie a holiday ribbon around each glass stem and knot miniature Christmas ornaments onto the ribbon ends.

In a medium saucepan, combine caramel bits and $^1/_4$ cup evaporated milk. Stirring constantly, cook over low heat until caramels are melted. Remove from heat and set aside.

Combine remaining $^1/_4$ cup milk, cake mix, butter, and vanilla; stir until blended. Spread half of batter into a foil-lined, lightly greased 9-inch square baking pan. Bake at 350° for 10 minutes; cool pan on a wire rack 5 minutes. Pour caramel mixture over baked brownie layer; sprinkle with walnuts. Spoon remaining batter over walnuts. Bake at 350° for 25 minutes; cool completely in pan on a wire rack. Cover and chill brownies before cutting into 1 x 2-inch bars.

Yield: 32 brownies

Chocolate Caramel Brownies
and Pumpkin Tiramisu

Pumpkin Tiramisu
Filling
- 1½ cups whipping cream
- ¾ cup sugar
- 1 container (8 ounces) mascarpone cheese
- 1 can (15 ounces) pumpkin
- ½ teaspoon ground cinnamon
- ¼ teaspoon ground cloves
- ¼ teaspoon ground ginger
- 2 packages (6.15 ounces each) halved ladyfingers
- ¼ cup orange liqueur, divided

Topping
- 1½ cups whipping cream
- 6 tablespoons powdered sugar
- 2 tablespoons orange liqueur
- 1 teaspoon vanilla extract
- 1 cup crushed amaretti cookies

For filling, beat whipping cream and sugar in a large bowl until peaks form. Add mascarpone cheese, pumpkin, and spices; beat just until smooth.

Line bottom of a 9-inch springform pan with 1 package of the ladyfingers, overlapping to fit. Sprinkle with 2 tablespoons orange liqueur. Spread half of filling over ladyfingers. Repeat with remaining ladyfingers, orange liqueur, and filling. Smooth top and tightly wrap in plastic wrap; chill overnight.

To unmold; run knife around inside edge of pan. Release pan sides and transfer tiramisu to a serving plate.

For topping, beat whipping cream, powdered sugar, orange liqueur, and vanilla in a large bowl until peaks form. Spread over top of tiramisu. Press crushed cookies onto sides and sprinkle on top.
Yield: 8 servings

Begin a *New* Tradition

The first Sunday in December, our town hosts a Christmas Parade that passes by our house. We have an open house party, and when the parade ends, I serve a big lunch with all the trimmings. After that, I play the piano and we have a traditional sing-along. One year, our house was one of seven homes selected to host a Holiday House Tour to help cover parade expenses. I decorated every room with snowmen and served cookies and punch. I was delighted when our house was voted the best-decorated.

Jo Ann V. Noble
Merrimac, MA

Gingerbread-Apple Upside-Down Cake
- 4 large Granny Smith apples, peeled, cored, and sliced
- 2 tablespoons freshly squeezed lemon juice
- ¾ cup butter, softened and divided
- 6 tablespoons sugar, divided
- 6 tablespoons apple cider
- 1 cup all-purpose flour
- 1 tablespoon ground ginger
- 1 teaspoon ground cinnamon
- ¼ teaspoon ground cloves
- ¼ teaspoon ground nutmeg
- ¼ teaspoon salt
- ¼ cup firmly packed brown sugar
- 3 eggs
- ½ cup molasses
- 2 tablespoons boiling water
- 1 teaspoon baking soda

Grease an 8-inch square baking pan; set aside.

In a large bowl, stir apples with lemon juice; set aside. In a large skillet, melt ¼ cup butter with ¼ cup sugar. Add apples to skillet and stirring constantly, cook 3 to 4 minutes or until browned. Transfer apples to a plate. Add apple cider and remaining 2 tablespoons sugar to juices in skillet. Stirring constantly, cook about 1 minute or until mixture becomes a syrup consistency. Pour syrup into prepared baking pan; swirl to coat bottom. Arrange apple slices in a single layer over syrup; set aside.

In a medium bowl, combine flour, ginger, cinnamon, cloves, nutmeg, and salt. In a large bowl, combine remaining ½ cup butter and brown sugar; beat until fluffy. Add eggs and molasses; beat until well combined. Add half of the flour mixture; beat until well blended. In a small bowl, combine baking soda and boiling water; beat into batter. Add remaining flour mixture; beat until well combined.

Pour batter over apples in pan, being careful to prevent apple slices from moving. Bake at 350° for 25 minutes; reduce heat to 325° and bake 10 to 15 minutes more or until a toothpick inserted in center comes out clean. Cool on a wire rack 1 hour. Run a knife between cake and pan; invert onto a serving plate.
Yield: 8 servings

White Chocolate-Pistachio Mini Cheesecakes

Crust
- 1/2 cup butter, softened
- 1/3 cup sugar
- 1 teaspoon vanilla extract
- 1 1/4 cups all-purpose flour
- 1/2 cup finely chopped pistachios

Filling
- 2 packages (8 ounces each) cream cheese, softened
- 2/3 cup sugar
- 2 eggs
- 1 teaspoon vanilla extract
- 4 ounces white baking chocolate, melted and cooled

Topping
- 1/2 cup butter, softened
- 1 1/2 cups powdered sugar
- 1 teaspoon vanilla extract
- 2 ounces white baking chocolate, melted and cooled
- 1/4 cup chopped pistachios

For crust, cream butter, sugar, and vanilla in a medium bowl until fluffy. Add flour; stir until well blended. Stir in pistachios. Press 1 teaspoon of crust mixture into bottom of each paper-lined cup of a miniature muffin pan.

For filling, beat cream cheese and sugar in a medium bowl until fluffy. Add eggs and vanilla; beat until well blended. Stir in white chocolate. Spoon 1 tablespoon filling over each crust. Bake at 350° for 13 to 16 minutes or until filling is set in center. Place pan on a wire rack to cool.

For topping, beat butter, powdered sugar, and vanilla until fluffy. Stir in chocolate. Spoon into a decorating bag fitted with a large star tip. Pipe topping on each cheesecake. Sprinkle with chopped pistachios. Store in refrigerator.

Yield: about 5 dozen cheesecakes

Toasted Coconut-Rum Cupcakes

Cupcakes
- 1 package (18.25 ounces) white cake mix
- 1 cup cream of coconut
- 1/4 cup vegetable oil
- 1/4 cup dark rum
- 4 eggs

Frosting
- 2 cups whipping cream
- 1/2 cup cream of coconut
- 6 tablespoons powdered sugar
- 1 tablespoon dark rum
- 1 can (3.5 ounces) shredded coconut, toasted

For cupcakes, combine cake mix, cream of coconut, vegetable oil, rum, and eggs in a large bowl; beat 2 to 3 minutes or until well blended. Spoon batter into paper-lined muffin cups, filling 2/3 full. Bake at 350° for 15 to 18 minutes or until a toothpick inserted into centers comes out clean. Cool completely on a wire rack.

For frosting, combine whipping cream, cream of coconut, powdered sugar, and rum in a large bowl; beat until peaks form. Spread frosting onto cupcakes; sprinkle with toasted coconut.

Yield: 2 dozen cupcakes

White Chocolate-Pistachio Mini Cheesecakes

Almond Cream Puffs

Almond Cream Puffs
Filling
- 2 cups whipping cream
- 1/2 cup powdered sugar
- 1/4 cup Instant cheesecake pudding mix
- 1/2 teaspoon almond extract

Puffs
- 1 cup water
- 1/2 cup butter
- 1/2 teaspoon salt
- 1 cup all-purpose flour
- 4 eggs
- Garnish: powdered sugar and sliced almonds, toasted

For filling, combine whipping cream, powdered sugar, pudding mix, and almond extract in a large bowl. Beat on high speed until thick and fluffy. Refrigerate until ready to use.

For puffs, preheat oven to 400°. In a large saucepan, combine water, butter, and salt; bring to a boil. Add flour to boiling mixture and stir vigorously until mixture leaves sides of pan. Remove from heat and cool slightly, about 5 minutes. Add eggs, one at a time, stirring until mixture is smooth. Drop by 1/4 cupfuls onto a parchment-lined baking sheet, 2 inches apart, piling dough slightly in center. Bake 30 minutes, reduce heat to 350°, and continue to bake 10 minutes more. After puffs are cool, cut off tops, spoon 1/2 cup filling onto each puff, replace top, and sprinkle with powdered sugar and toasted sliced almonds.
Yield: 8 puffs

Remember . . .

if you're worried about getting candle wax on your favorite tablecloth, battery-powered candles are a good alternative. Decorative hollow candles that can be refilled with smaller candles are also available. On a buffet table, position candles so guests won't have to reach over them.

Wine Punch
- 1 bottle (1.5 liters) white wine, chilled
- 1 bottle (32 ounces) cranberry juice cocktail, chilled
- 1 can (12 ounces) frozen pineapple juice concentrate
- 1 can (12 ounces) frozen pink lemonade concentrate
- 6 cups lemon-lime soda, chilled

In a punch bowl, combine wine, cranberry juice cocktail, and concentrates. To serve, stir in lemon-lime soda. Serve chilled.
Yield: about twenty-four 6-ounce servings

Eggnog Trifle

   2 cups eggnog
   1 package (3.4 ounces) instant vanilla pudding mix
   1 container (16 ounces) frozen whipped topping, thawed and divided
   1 frozen pound cake (16 ounces), thawed, cut into cubes, and divided
   2 tablespoons amaretto, divided
   2 packages (6 ounces each) fresh raspberries, divided
 3/4 cup shredded coconut, toasted and divided

   Beat eggnog and pudding for 3 minutes. Fold in half of whipped topping. Chill until set.
   Place half of pound cake cubes in a 14-cup trifle bowl. Sprinkle with 1 tablespoon amaretto. Layer with half of raspberries, half of eggnog mixture, and 1/2 cup of coconut. Layer with remaining pound cake, amaretto, raspberries (reserving a few raspberries for garnish), and remaining eggnog mixture. Garnish with remaining whipped topping, coconut, and raspberries.
Yield: 14 servings

Holiday Punch

   1 can (46 ounces) unsweetened pineapple juice, chilled
   2 cups piña colada drink mixer, chilled
   1 can (12 ounces) frozen orange juice concentrate, thawed
   1 liter club soda, chilled
   1 liter lemon-lime soda, chilled
   1 package (10 ounces) frozen raspberries in syrup, slightly thawed

   In a punch bowl, stir together pineapple juice, piña colada mixer, orange juice, club soda, and lemon-lime soda. To serve, stir in raspberries. Serve chilled.
Yield: about twenty-four 6-ounce servings

Chocolate Dipped Biscotti

- 1/2 cup butter or margarine, softened
- 1 cup sugar
- 2 eggs
- 1 teaspoon vanilla extract
- 2 1/4 cups all-purpose flour
- 1/4 cup cocoa
- 1 teaspoon baking powder
- 1/2 teaspoon baking soda
- 1/4 teaspoon salt
- 3 containers (7 ounces each) microwaveable dipping chocolate

In a large bowl, cream butter and sugar until fluffy. Add eggs and vanilla; beat until smooth. In a medium bowl, combine flour, cocoa, baking powder, baking soda, and salt. Add dry ingredients to creamed mixture; stir until a soft dough forms. Divide dough into thirds. Shape each piece of dough into a 2 x 9-inch loaf, flouring hands as necessary. Allow 3 inches between loaves on a greased and floured baking sheet. Bake at 375° for 18 to 22 minutes or until loaves are firm. Cool 10 minutes on baking sheet.

Cut loaves diagonally into 1/2 inch slices. Lay slices flat on an ungreased baking sheet. Bake 5 minutes; turn slices over and bake 5 minutes longer. Transfer cookies to a wire rack to cool. Dip cooled biscotti into melted chocolate. Place on wax paper-lined baking sheet to allow chocolate to harden. Store in an airtight container.

Yield: about 4 dozen cookies

Remember . . .

tiny bottles of coffee syrup, tied with festive ribbons and gift tags, make memorable party favors. Or for Old World charm, give each guest a wax stamping set for sealing their correspondence.

Party Favor Candles and Hostess Book

Invite each guest to sign your hostess book upon arrival and take a favor as they depart. Instructions are on pages 146 and 147.

Special guests deserve special treatment. Pamper them with a coffee bar stocked with cream, sugar cubes, finely ground cinnamon, and chocolate shavings. Add a couple of home-brewed syrups and flavorings, and the java aficionados in your crowd will be sure to mark their calendars for your event next year.

Gingerbread Spice Coffee Syrup

This syrup is also good on hot cereals, pancakes, or waffles.

- 1 cup water
- 1 cup sugar
- 1 tablespoon honey
- 1 piece (one inch) fresh ginger root, sliced
- 1 whole cinnamon stick, broken into pieces
- 8 whole cloves
- 1/2 teaspoon whole allspice
- 1/2 teaspoon whole peppercorns
- 1/2 teaspoon ground nutmeg

Combine water, sugar, and honey in a saucepan. Stir in remaining ingredients and bring to a boil. Reduce heat and simmer for 30 minutes. Strain mixture.
Yield: about 1³/₄ cups syrup

Vanilla Bean Coffee Syrup

- 2 cups sugar
- 2 cups water
- 1 vanilla bean

Combine sugar and water in a saucepan. Split vanilla bean, scrape seeds into pan, and add pod. Bring mixture to a boil, reduce heat and simmer for about 20 minutes or until volume is reduced in half. Strain mixture.
Yield: 2 cups syrup

Coffee Syrup Labels
Make labels for your favorite coffee
syrups. Instructions are on page 146.

Chocolate Caramel Coffee Syrup

1 cup whipping cream
1 cup light corn syrup
1/2 cup granulated sugar
1/2 cup firmly packed brown
   sugar
1/8 teaspoon salt
4 ounces milk chocolate,
   chopped
1/4 cup butter

Combine cream, corn syrup, sugars, and salt in a saucepan. Bring to a boil over medium heat; cook 5 minutes, stirring constantly. Remove from heat and stir in chocolate and butter, stirring until mixture is smooth.
Yield: 2 cups syrup

Remember . . .

Among the numerous luxuries of the table ...coffee may be considered as one of the most valuable. It excites cheerfulness without intoxication; and the pleasing flow of spirits which it occasions...is never followed by sadness, languor or debility.

Benjamin Franklin

During the holidays, physical distances disappear. Aunts and Uncles, siblings and cousins—when it's time to sit down together for Christmas dinner, everyone who can possibly be there is there. Gentle teasings and corny jokes are passed around the table with the cranberry salad. Old traditions shine again. Youngsters discover family lore. And Christmas dishes are introduced—eventually, some of these will also be traditions. But for right now, it's enough just to savor the warmth of being together around a meal prepared with love.

The best judges of a holiday recipe's success are the people who gather at your Christmas dinner table year after year. While longstanding recipes like Great-Grandmother Inez's sweet potatoes or Uncle John's black-eyed pea salad will always be served, each generation of cooks will also bring something new to the table. And perhaps that is the best part of being a holiday chef—knowing that a dish you introduce will forever be known by your name.

Cranberry-Champagne Cocktails

1 quart cranberry juice cocktail, chilled
1 bottle (750 ml) champagne, chilled

Combine ingredients in a 2-quart pitcher; stir until blended. Serve chilled.
Yield: about nine 6-ounce servings

Cranberry Salad

2 boxes (0.3 ounces each) sugar-free black cherry gelatin
1 cup sugar
2 cups hot water
1 cup cold water
1 package (12 ounces) fresh cranberries, coarsely chopped
1 can (10.5 ounce) mandarin oranges, drained
1/2 cup chopped pecans, toasted
Leafy green lettuce
Garnish: Sweetened Whipped Cream (recipe on page 121)

Place gelatin and sugar in a medium bowl. Stir in hot water, stirring until gelatin and sugar dissolve. Stir in cold water; cool. Place mixture in refrigerator until slightly set. Stir in cranberries, mandarin oranges, and pecans. Pour into desired mold (we used 1/2-cup star-shaped molds). Refrigerate until ready to serve.

To serve, unmold salad onto a plate lined with lettuce. Garnish with a dollop of Sweetened Whipped Cream, if desired.
Yield: 6 servings

Curried Butternut Squash Soup

2 small acorn squash
1/2 cup salted butter
8 ounces sliced fresh mushrooms
1 can (32 ounces) low sodium chicken broth
2 packages (8 ounces each) frozen puréed butternut squash or one large butternut squash, peeled, seeded, and cut into cubes
1 cup chopped carrot
1/2 cup chopped onion
2 tablespoons curry powder or to taste
Ground sea salt
White pepper

Wash acorn squash. Cut in half and scrape out seeds. Place face down in a microwave-safe baking dish; add water to come halfway up squash. Microwave on HIGH 5 minutes or until tender. Scoop out inside of squash into a 4-quart slow cooker.

Melt butter in a large skillet. Add mushrooms and cook 10 minutes or until soft. Add mushrooms to slow cooker along with remaining ingredients. Cook on HIGH 20 minutes, then on LOW for 1 hour; cool slightly. Remove solid ingredients and purée in a food processor or blender. Add mixture back into slow cooker and stir until well blended. Cook on HIGH until heated through.
Yield: about 8 servings

Light Yeast Biscuits

1 package dry yeast
2 tablespoons warm water
2 tablespoons sugar, divided
2 1/2 cups all-purpose flour
1/2 teaspoon baking powder
1/2 teaspoon baking soda
1/2 teaspoon salt
1/2 cup butter or margarine, softened
1 cup warm buttermilk
Vegetable cooking spray

In a small bowl, dissolve yeast in warm water; stir in 1 tablespoon sugar. In a large bowl, combine remaining 1 tablespoon sugar, flour, baking powder, baking soda, and salt. Using a pastry blender, cut butter into dry ingredients until mixture is crumbly. Add buttermilk and yeast mixture to dry ingredients; stir until a soft dough forms. Turn onto a lightly floured surface and knead 4 minutes or until dough becomes smooth and elastic. Place in a large bowl sprayed with cooking spray, turning once to coat top of dough. Cover and let rise in a warm place (80 to 85°) 1 to 1 1/2 hours or until doubled in size. Turn dough onto a lightly floured surface and punch down. Roll out dough to 1/2-inch thickness; use 2-inch-diameter biscuit cutter to cut out biscuits. Place 1 inch apart on an ungreased baking sheet. Spray tops with cooking spray, cover, and let rise in a warm place 30 to 45 minutes or until doubled in size. Bake at 400° for 12 to 15 minutes or until golden brown. Serve warm.
Yield: about 2 dozen biscuits

Remember . . .

if your family's Christmas celebration includes a reading from the Bible or *The Night Before Christmas*, videotape the event and make copies of the video for the children. When the kids grow up and move away, they'll always have those early memories to cherish.

Glazed Carrots and Pearl Onions

1 package (16 ounces) peeled baby carrots
1 can (14 ounces) chicken broth
2 cups (half of a 16-ounce bag) frozen white pearl onions
6 tablespoons butter
1/4 cup sugar
2 tablespoons chopped fresh parsley
1 teaspoon salt
2 tablespoons cornstarch
2 tablespoons cold water

Remember...

to eat a Cornish hen, cut it apart as you would a large bird, removing one drumstick before cutting into the breast; then, repeat on the remaining side.

Combine carrots and chicken broth in a large saucepan. Bring to a boil; reduce to a simmer and cover. Cook 5 minutes. Add onions, butter, sugar, parsley, and salt. Cook about 3 minutes more or until carrots and onions are tender. Combine cornstarch and water in a small bowl, stirring until cornstarch dissolves. Stir mixture into saucepan and bring to a boil; cook 1 minute more or until sauce thickens.
Yield: 4 cups vegetables

Wild Rice and Cranberry Dressing

- ½ cup butter or margarine
- 1½ cups chopped onions
- ¾ cup thinly sliced celery
- 2 garlic cloves, minced
- 1 package (6 ounces) wild rice
- ½ teaspoon dried thyme leaves
- ½ teaspoon dried sage leaves
- ½ teaspoon salt
- ½ teaspoon black pepper
- 3 cans (14½ ounces each) chicken broth
- 1 package (16 ounces) brown rice
- 1 package (6 ounces) sweetened dried cranberries
- ½ cup chopped fresh parsley
- 1 cup coarsely chopped pecans, toasted

In a Dutch oven, melt butter over medium heat. Sauté onions, celery, and garlic until tender. Stir in wild rice, thyme, sage, salt, and pepper. Add chicken broth; bring to a boil. Reduce heat to low; cover and simmer 30 minutes. Stir in brown rice; cover and simmer another 30 minutes. Stir in cranberries and parsley; cover and simmer 20 minutes longer or until broth is absorbed and brown rice is done. Stir in pecans. Serve warm.
Yield: about 10 cups dressing

Parmesan Spinach and Artichokes

- ½ cup chopped green onions
- ½ cup chopped celery
- ½ cup butter or margarine
- 2 packages (10 ounces each) frozen chopped spinach, cooked and drained
- 2 cups sour cream
- 1 can (14 ounces) artichoke hearts, drained and chopped
- ½ teaspoon hot pepper sauce
- ½ teaspoon salt
- ¼ teaspoon black pepper
- 8 ounces bacon, cooked, crumbled, and divided
- ½ cup freshly shredded Parmesan cheese

In a small saucepan over medium heat, cook onions and celery in butter until vegetables are tender. In a greased 2-quart baking dish, combine onion mixture, and next 6 ingredients. Reserving 2 tablespoons bacon for garnish, stir remaining bacon into spinach mixture. Sprinkle cheese over top of casserole. Bake at 350° for 30 to 40 minutes or until edges are lightly browned and mixture is heated through. Garnish with reserved bacon.
Yield: about 8 to 10 servings

Cornish Hens with Citrus Glaze

- 6 Cornish hens (22 ounces each)
- Vegetable oil
- Citrus Glaze (recipe follows)
- Garnish: orange slices

Remove giblets, and then place hens, breast side up, in shallow roasting pans; tie legs together, if desired. Lightly brush hens with vegetable oil. Bake at 375° for 1½ hours, brushing with glaze every 30 minutes. Hens are done when a thermometer inserted in the thickest part of thigh registers 180°. Garnish with orange slices, if desired.
Yield: 6 servings

Citrus Glaze

- ⅔ cup sugar
- ¾ cup orange juice
- 2 tablespoons butter
- 2 tablespoons lemon juice

Combine sugar and orange juice in a small saucepan, and bring to a boil; remove from heat. Add butter and lemon juice; stir until butter is melted.
Yield: about 1¼ cups glaze

Begin a New Tradition

My favorite event of Christmas is a Madrigal dinner hosted by a local university each year. It's always at the beginning of the season. The members of the choir dress in Renaissance attire and serve a traditional holiday meal accompanied by hymns. Between courses, the singers give amusing toasts. I was first invited to attend this event with a friend several years ago, and I still love to go every year—it starts out the holidays in the right spirit.

Laura Holyfield
Little Rock, Arkansas

Sticky Date Pudding

A cake that comes to us from Australia.

1 package (10 ounces) chopped dates
2 teaspoons baking soda
1 cup butter, softened
1/2 cup sugar
4 eggs
2 1/2 cups all-purpose flour
1 teaspoon salt
1 tablespoon vanilla extract
2 teaspoons baking powder
Caramel Sauce (recipe follows)

Cover dates with water in a saucepan and bring to a boil. Reduce heat and simmer for about 3 minutes; add baking soda. Cool and drain, reserving 1 cup of the liquid. Cream butter and sugar. Beat in eggs, one at a time, beating well after each addition. Combine flour, salt, and baking powder; stir into butter mixture. Stir in vanilla, date liquid, and dates until well combined. Pour into a greased 8-inch square baking pan. Bake at 350° for 40 minutes or until top is lightly browned and center is barely set. Cut into squares and serve warm with Caramel Sauce.
Yield: 16 servings

Caramel Sauce
1 cup firmly packed brown sugar
1/2 cup whipping cream
1/2 cup butter
2 tablespoons dark rum

Combine all the ingredients in a saucepan over medium heat, stirring constantly until smooth. Serve warm over cake.
Yield: 1 3/4 cups sauce

Pecan-Cream Cheese Pie
4 eggs, divided
1/3 plus 1/2 cup sugar, divided
1 package (8 ounces) cream cheese, softened
2 teaspoons vanilla extract, divided
1 unbaked 9-inch pie shell
1 1/4 cups pecan halves
1 cup light corn syrup

Beat together 1 egg, 1/3 cup sugar, cream cheese, and 1 teaspoon vanilla until well blended; pour into pie crust. Sprinkle pecans over mixture. Beat remaining 3 eggs, remaining 1/2 cup sugar, corn syrup, and remaining 1 teaspoon vanilla until well blended; pour over pecans. Bake at 375° for 50 minutes or until center is set.
Yield: 8 servings

Christmas morning.

Bits of wrapping paper, curls of ribbon, flattened stockings—the happy aftermath of Christmas morning has arrived. About mid-morning, everyone remembers they skipped breakfast. But you were anticipating that moment. Cranberry-Walnut Coffee Cake, Cheesy Egg Casserole, or Sausage-Pineapple Pastries are ready to heap up on the plates of your pajama-clad crew.

Christmas has come at last. And all of it, from the first card mailed out to the last gift placed under the tree, has been just as you wanted it to be. So help yourself to another piece of Caramelized Bacon. Savor the season. And know that next year, it's going to be even better.

Cranberry-Walnut Coffee Cake

Baked Fruit Casserole

- 1 can (15 ounces) dark sweet cherries
- 1 cup firmly packed brown sugar
- 1/4 cup butter or margarine
- 2 tablespoons cornstarch
- 1/8 teaspoon salt
- Juice and grated zest of 1 orange
- Juice and grated zest of 1 lemon
- 1 can (20 ounces) pineapple chunks, drained
- 1 can (15 ounces) peach halves, drained
- 1 can (15 ounces) apricot halves, drained

In a medium saucepan, combine juice from cherries, brown sugar, butter, cornstarch, and salt. Add juice and zest from orange and lemon. Stirring constantly, cook over medium heat until mixture thickens; set aside. Place fruit in a greased 2-quart casserole dish; pour juice mixture over fruit. Bake at 350° for 30 minutes or until fruit is hot.

Yield: about 6 cups fruit

Potato Croquettes

- 9 medium red potatoes, peeled and quartered (about 3 1/2 pounds)
- 1/3 cup butter or margarine, softened
- 1/2 cup finely chopped green onions
- 3 eggs, beaten
- 1 teaspoon salt
- 1/4 teaspoon white pepper
- 1 cup purchased seasoned bread crumbs
- Vegetable oil

Boil potatoes until soft; drain. Beat potatoes and butter until smooth. Stir in onions, eggs, salt, and white pepper. Cool mixture until able to handle. For each patty, drop 1/3 cup potato mixture into bread crumbs and shape into a 3-inch diameter patty, covering with crumbs. In a large skillet, heat a thin layer of oil. Fry patties in oil until golden brown on both sides, adding oil as needed. Serve warm.

Yield: about 18 potato patties

Remember...

take advantage of make-ahead planning. Refrigerate the casseroles the night before and set the cake down from the freezer. If you'll have company, ask guests to bring a dish to add to the brunch. On Christmas Day, you'll want to relax with everyone else.

Cranberry-Walnut Coffee Cake

Cake
- 1 cup butter, softened
- 2 1/2 cups sugar
- 6 eggs
- 2/3 cup cranberry sauce
- 3 cups all-purpose flour
- 1 teaspoon baking soda
- 1 teaspoon ground cinnamon
- 1/2 teaspoon salt
- 1/2 cup sour cream
- 1 cup sweetened dried cranberries
- 3/4 cup chopped walnuts
- 1 teaspoon orange zest

Streusel
- 1 cup chopped walnuts
- 1 cup firmly packed brown sugar
- 1/4 cup all-purpose flour
- 1 teaspoon ground cinnamon
- 3 tablespoons butter, softened

Glaze
- 1 cup powdered sugar
- 4 to 5 teaspoons orange juice
- Garnish: sweetened dried cranberries

Grease and flour a 10-inch tube pan; set aside.

For cake, combine butter and sugar in a large mixing bowl; beat until fluffy. Add eggs, one at a time, beating well after each addition. Add cranberry sauce and beat until smooth. In a medium bowl, combine flour, baking soda, cinnamon, and salt. Add half of flour mixture to butter mixture and beat until combined. Stir in sour cream then remaining flour mixture; beat until smooth. Stir in cranberries, walnuts, and orange zest; set aside.

For streusel, combine walnuts, brown sugar, flour, and cinnamon in a small bowl. Cut in butter until mixture resembles coarse crumbs. Spoon half of cake batter into prepared pan. Sprinkle one cup of streusel over batter. Repeat with remaining batter and streusel. Bake at 325° for 1 1/2 hours or until a toothpick inserted in center comes out clean, covering with foil last 30 minutes of baking. Transfer pan to a wire rack to cool completely; remove cake from pan.

For glaze, combine powdered sugar and orange juice in a small bowl; stir until smooth. Transfer coffee cake to a serving plate and drizzle with glaze. Garnish with cranberries, if desired.

Yield: 16 servings

Caramelized Bacon

1 package (12 ounces) sliced, center-cut bacon
1 cup firmly packed brown sugar
1 tablespoon ground cinnamon

Cut bacon slices in half. Combine sugar and cinnamon; generously coat bacon on both sides with the sugar mixture. Arrange bacon in a single layer on a foil-lined jellyroll pan or broiler pan; sprinkle with any remaining sugar. Bake at 350° for 15 to 20 minutes, or until bacon is crisp. Immediately transfer bacon onto foil to cool slightly. Serve warm.

Yield: about 38 pieces bacon

Cheesy Egg Casserole

Assemble casserole the night before.

2 tablespoons butter or margarine, softened
6 slices white bread, crusts removed
1/3 cup finely chopped green onions
1 tablespoon vegetable oil
9 eggs
2 1/2 cups half and half
2 cans (7 ounces each) mushroom pieces, drained
1 can (4.5 ounces) chopped green chiles, drained
1 1/4 teaspoons salt
1/8 teaspoon ground black pepper
2 cups (8 ounces) shredded Monterey Jack cheese, divided

Spread butter over bread slices. Place in bottom of a greased 9 x 13-inch baking dish. In a small skillet, sauté green onions in oil over medium heat until tender. Beat eggs in a medium bowl. Stir onions, half and half, mushrooms, green chiles, salt, and black pepper into eggs. Stir in 1 1/2 cups cheese. Pour egg mixture over bread slices. Cover and chill overnight.

Sprinkle remaining 1/2 cup cheese over casserole. Bake at 350° for 45 minutes or until egg mixture is set. Serve warm.

Yield: about 12 servings

Sausage-Pineapple Pastries

Pastries can be made ahead, covered with plastic wrap, and refrigerated until ready to bake.

1 pound mild pork sausage
1/2 cup chopped onion
2/3 cup pineapple preserves
1 tablespoon dry mustard
1/2 teaspoon salt
1/4 teaspoon black pepper
1/8 teaspoon rubbed sage
1 package (15 ounces) refrigerated pie crusts, at room temperature

In a large skillet, cook sausage until it begins to brown; drain well. Add onion; cook until onion is tender and sausage is thoroughly cooked. Remove from heat. Stir in preserves, dry mustard, salt, pepper, and sage; set aside.

Working with one pie crust at a time, cut out individual pastries using a 3-inch star-shaped cookie cutter on a lightly floured surface. Using a floured rolling pin, roll and cut out dough scraps. Place stars into lightly greased miniature muffin pans. Spoon 1 scant tablespoon sausage mixture into each pastry. Bake at 400° for 9 to 11 minutes or until crust is lightly browned. Serve warm.

Yield: about 3 1/2 dozen pastries

Here's How

Supply Scape
(from page 114)

This centerpiece is an artful combination of form and function.

1. For the table runner, measure the length of the table and add 24". Cut four 4"w ribbon lengths this measurement. Removing the wires where the ribbon edges overlap, zigzag the ribbons together along the long edges. Notch the ends to complete the ribbon runner.

2. For the centerpiece, fill glass vases with ornaments. Set each vase on a base and tie 1½"w ribbon around each one.

3. Punch tags from different colors of cardstock and add ¼"w ribbon ties. Arrange the tags in the footed bowl. Place the bowl and some jingle bells on the runner.

4. Add several Ribbon Holders to complete the supply scape.

• 4"w dupioni silk wire-edged ribbon • three large glass vases with bases • different-sized red, gold, and green glass ornaments • 1½"w ribbon • tag-shaped punches and hole punch • cardstock • ¼"w ribbons • footed glass bowl • extra large jingle bells with striped ribbon ties • Ribbon Holders (next page)

Ribbon Holders

(from page 114)

You and your guests will love these handy ribbon holders. To get started, gather several spools of ribbon and purchase the largest diameter dowel rods that will fit through the spools.

1. Spray paint each wood base and dowel rod and allow to dry. Stack the ribbon spools according to each color family. Cut a rod 1" longer than each stack.

2. Drill a dowel-size hole into the center of each base. To prevent the dowel from splitting when attaching the drawer pull, pre-drill a small hole in the center of one end of each dowel. Glue and insert the other end of the dowel in a base. Thread spools on the dowel and attach the drawer pull.

- spray paint • wood bases • dowel rods • different-colored ribbon spools • small-toothed handsaw • drill • wood glue • glass drawer pull

Wrapping Ideas

(from page 115)

Add to the celebration with easy embellishments for your wrapped presents. Here are some ideas to get you started.

Package A. Add a decorative rub-on to a punched round cardstock tag (we found one that coordinates with the pattern on our ribbon) and write a message along the edge. Add a gilded edge and highlights with a glue pen and glitter. Shake off the excess glitter onto a paper plate. Tie the tag to a floral-shaped bow.

Package B. Tie a glittered feather to a ribbon knot and label one corner of the package with a glue pen and glitter.

Package C. Tie wire-edged ribbon around the package. Scrunch up the streamers for texture and attach a jingle bell.

Package D. Punch the corners from a square cardstock tag and add a message to the back. Stamp a design on the tag and sprinkle glitter on the wet ink. Shake off the excess glitter onto a paper plate. Using a piece of tape like a hinge, adhere the tag to the present next to a tailored ribbon bow.

Package E. Punch the corners from a square cardstock tag. Cut a slit near the side edges of the tag the width of your ribbon. Rub an initial on the tag and add swirls with a glue pen and glitter. Layer ribbons and thread them through the tag slits. Tape the ribbon ends to the bottom of the present.

- wrapped presents • rub-on designs and initials • tag-shaped punches, hole, and corner punches • cardstock • fine-point permanent pen • glue pen • fine glitter • paper plate • assorted ribbons • glittered feather • wire-edged ribbon • large jingle bell • rubber stamp • ink pad • transparent tape • craft knife and cutting mat

Wrapping Kits

(from page 113)

Wrap up a kit for each of your guests to use at the party, then to keep as a favor.

1. For each favor, wrap the box and lid with wrapping papers.

2. Cut a circle the size of the grommet hole through the center of the lid. Insert the grommet into the hole and turn the lid over. Use wire cutters to snip five or six times around the grommet post. Carefully hammer the grommet flat (Fig. 1).

3. Fold an 18" ribbon length in half and tie a knot near the fold. Thread the ends through the box lid from the back and notch the ends.

4. Fill each box with wrapping supplies.

Fig. 1

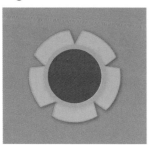

• papier-mâché boxes with lids (ours are 5" cubes) • wrapping papers • transparent tape • craft knife and cutting mat • large grommets or extra-large eyelets • wire cutters • hammer • 1¹/₂"w satin ribbon • wrapping supplies (such as small craft scissors, tape, glue pen, and glitter)

Dinner for Two Centerpiece

(from page 119)

Set the mood for a cozy dinner by the fireplace with elegant place settings and candlelight. For the centerpiece, add floral foam to the vase and bore a hole in the middle of the foam for the candle to rest in. Insert the candle in the foam. Spray the boxwood picks with glitter paint. When dry, arrange them around the candle. Attach each ornament to a pick. Insert the picks through the greenery into the foam and top off the arrangement with silver leaves.

• floral foam • vase or urn • craft knife • taper candle • glitter spray paint • boxwood picks • assorted ball ornaments • wired wood floral picks • glittered silver leaf picks

Mantel Decoration

(from page 118)

Coordinate the mantel and table arrangements to complete the romantic ambiance. Hot glue floral foam to the bottom of the urn and use floral tape to hold it tightly to the container. Bore three holes for the candles and insert them in the foam. Follow Dinner for Two Centerpiece instructions (previous page) to complete the urn. Extend the arrangement onto the mantel with more greenery and ornaments.

• hot glue gun • floral foam • urn • floral tape
• craft knife • three taper candles • glitter spray paint • boxwood picks • assorted ball ornaments
• wired wood floral picks • glittered silver leaf picks

Invitations

(from page 123)

These gorgeous invitations will set the tone for your holiday party and they are so simple to make. For each card, fold the short ends of a brown cardstock piece to meet in the middle and trim each end to a point. Type the invitation information to fit in a 3¹/₂" x 5" area and print it on cream cardstock. Leaving a blank space at the top for decoration, trim the invitation to fit the card. Glue sequins to the invitation in a wreath shape, glue the invitation to the card, and tie the card closed with ribbons. Mail the invitations in oversized envelopes or deliver them by hand.

• 5¹/₂" x 11" brown cardstock pieces
• cream-colored cardstock • craft glue
• leaf-shaped sequins • ¹/₄"w brown ribbons

145

Hostess Book

(from page 129)

Keep this book to gather your guests'
greetings at every holiday party.

1. Cut a fabric piece 1" larger on all sides
than the open book. Apply spray adhesive
on the wrong side of the fabric. Center the
open book on the fabric. Fold the fabric
corners diagonally over the book corners.
Smoothing the fabric as you go, fold the
short edges, then the long edges to the
inside of the book (trim the fabric at the
spine to fit).

2. Cut two 8" ribbon lengths. Glue one end
of each ribbon to the inside covers for ties.
Glue a non-fraying fabric piece to the inside
covers to hide the fabric and ribbon edges.

3. Tuck and glue the end of a ribbon length
between the spine and the pages at the
bottom to use as a bookmark. Run the
ribbon through the book and out the top.
Sew the ribbon end to the top of the tassel.

4. For gilded edges, hold the book closed
and buff the edges of the pages with
gold paste.

• fabric • small blank book • spray adhesive • ¼"w
ribbons • fabric glue • non-fraying fabric • tassel • soft
cloth • gold wax metallic finish paste

Coffee Syrup Labels

(from page 131)

We chose Amaretto and Irish Cream Syrups
in addition to the recipes given on pages
130 and 131. Choose an elegant font and
print the centered flavor names on cream
cardstock (we used 36 point Palace Script
MT font with 28 point line spacing for
ours). Then cut out the labels and round
the corners. Tape them to larger brown
background labels with rounded corners.
Run ribbon through slits cut near the sides
of each label and tape the ends at the back
of a cruet.

• cream and brown cardstock • corner
rounder punch • double-stick tape • brown
grosgrain ribbon • craft knife and cutting
mat • cruet for each syrup

Centerpiece
(from page 122)

For a splendid tablescape, paint the underside of clear glassware to complement amber candleholders and a bronze urn. (Painted glassware should not be heated in a microwave or oven and should be hand washed.)

1. For the centerpiece, fill the urn $2/3$ full of gravel. Trimming to fit, insert greenery stems in the urn, making sure the arrangement looks attractive from all sides. Next add the beaded picks, with taller stems in the center. Shape the leaves; then, cut them apart as desired and place them around the rim of the urn. Attach the bird ornaments to the greenery.

2. Lightly spray the backs of clear glass serving plates with wood tone spray (spray the backs only so food does not come in contact with the paint).

3. Masking the areas that aren't to be painted, spray paint the pedestals of the trifle bowl and biscotti bowl with gold paint, then wood tone spray.

4. Candles and wreaths placed around the urn and pedestals complete your elegant table.

• glass urn (ours has a bronze mirror-like finish) • pea gravel, kitty litter, or floral foam • wire cutters • glittered greenery picks • long gold beaded picks • glittered leaf picks • bird ornaments • clear glass plates • Design Master® Glossy Wood Tone Spray • masking tape and kraft paper • gold metallic spray paint • pedestal bowls for Eggnog Trifle and Chocolate Dipped Biscotti • candles • bay leaf wreaths

Party Favor Candles
(from page 129)

Give distinctive candle favors embellished with paper napkins, beads, and ribbon.

1. For each favor, cut a napkin slightly narrower than the height of the candle. Pull the layers apart and wrap the patterned piece around the candle. Trim the napkin so the ends overlap by $1/2$".

2. Slowly move the dryer set on hot (or the heat gun) back and forth along one section of the candle until the wax melts through. (If the candle begins dripping, let it cool a few seconds and roll the candle on a flat surface to press out the drips.) Continue a section at a time until the napkin ends overlap.

3. String a few beads on thread, running the thread around the end bead and back through the others to make a dangle. Tie ribbon around the candle and sew the dangle to the knot.

• patterned paper napkins • small pillar candles • hair dryer or heat gun • assorted glass beads • beading needle • thread • metallic mesh ribbon

Patterns

Elf Note
page 21

Roses on the Snow
page 62

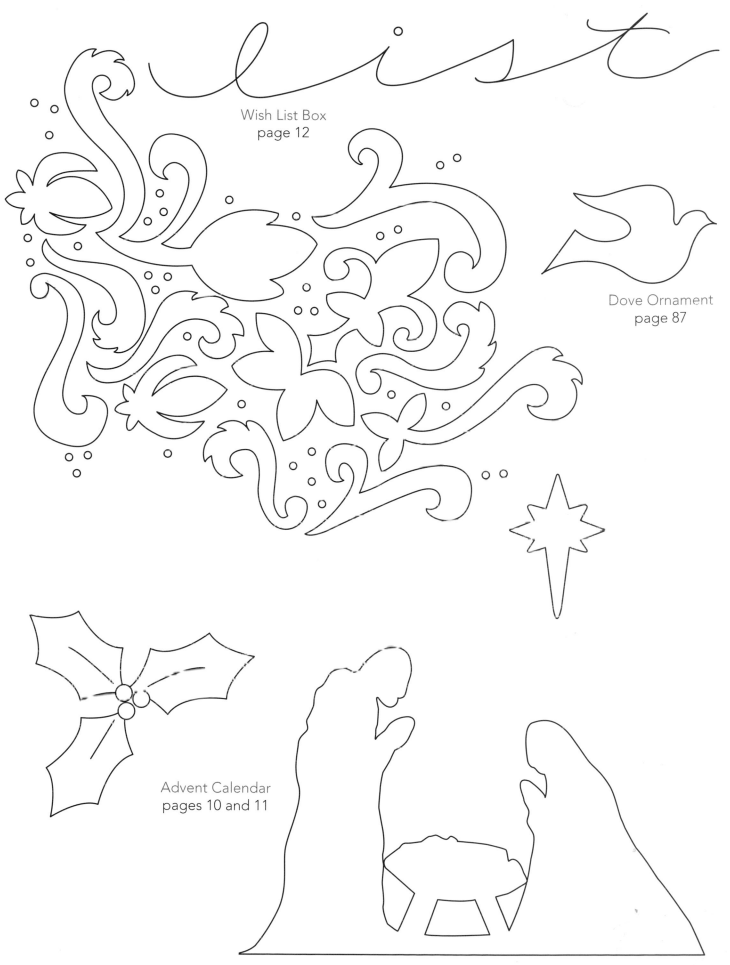

Wish List Box
page 12

Dove Ornament
page 87

Advent Calendar
pages 10 and 11

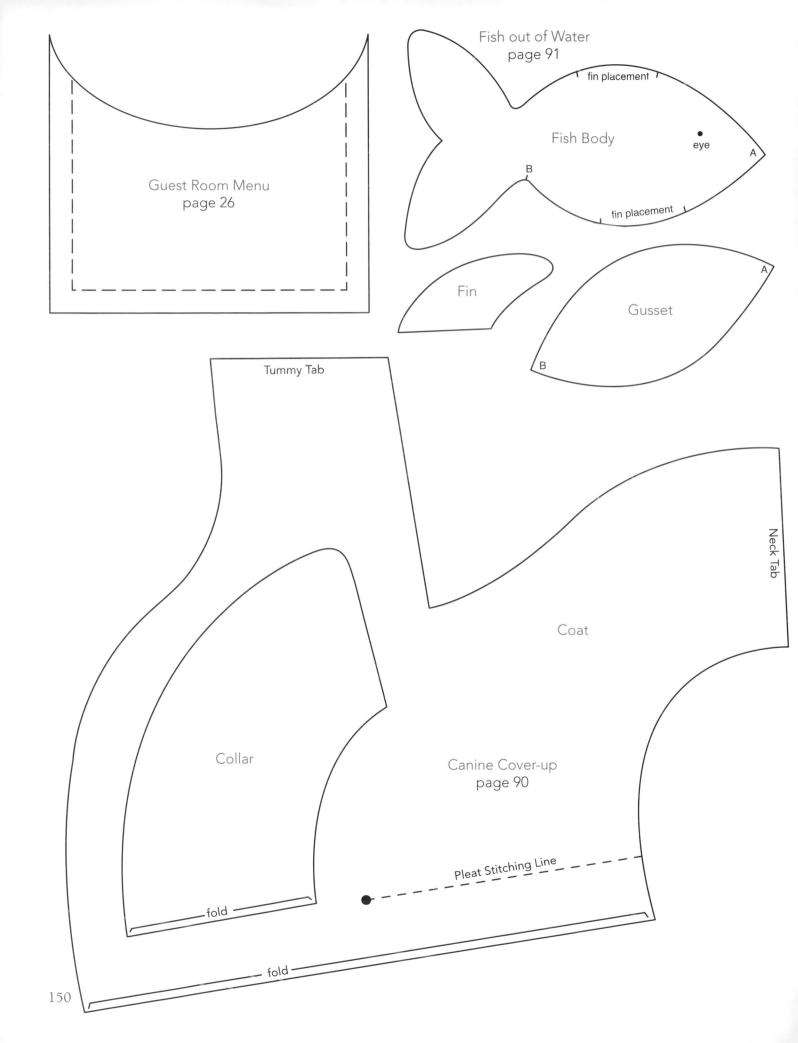

Guest Room Menu
page 26

Fish out of Water
page 91

fin placement

Fish Body

eye

A

B

fin placement

Fin

Gusset

A

B

Tummy Tab

Neck Tab

Coat

Collar

Canine Cover-up
page 90

Pleat Stitching Line

fold

fold

Appliqué Stockings
Floral Patterns
page 59

Christmas Card Box
page 17

Christmas Card Box
page 17

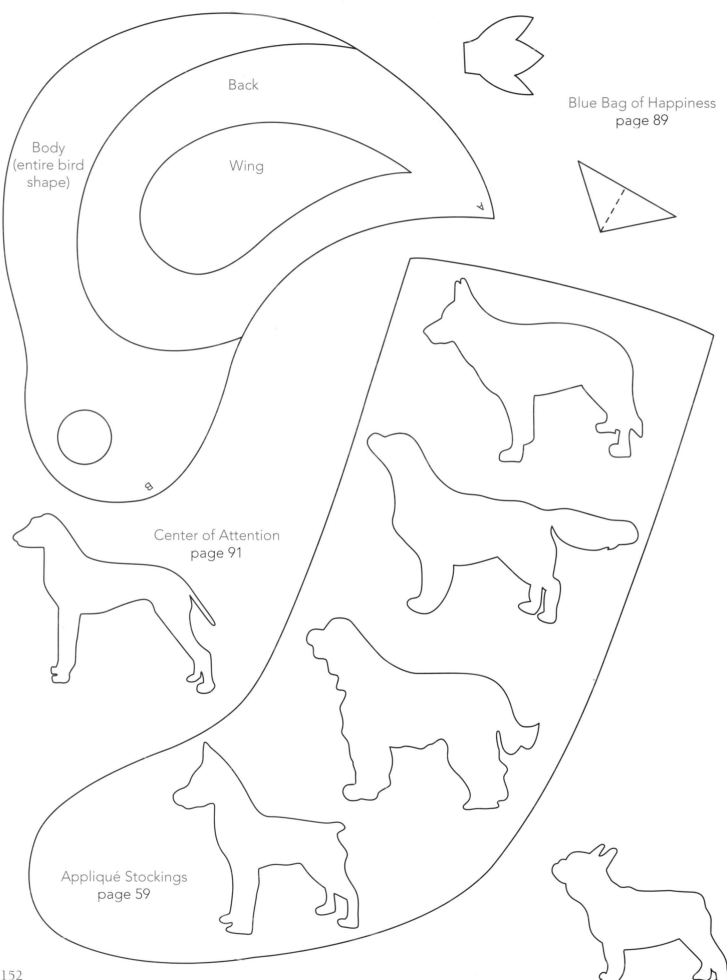

Back

Body
(entire bird
shape)

Wing

Blue Bag of Happiness
page 89

Center of Attention
page 91

Appliqué Stockings
page 59

152

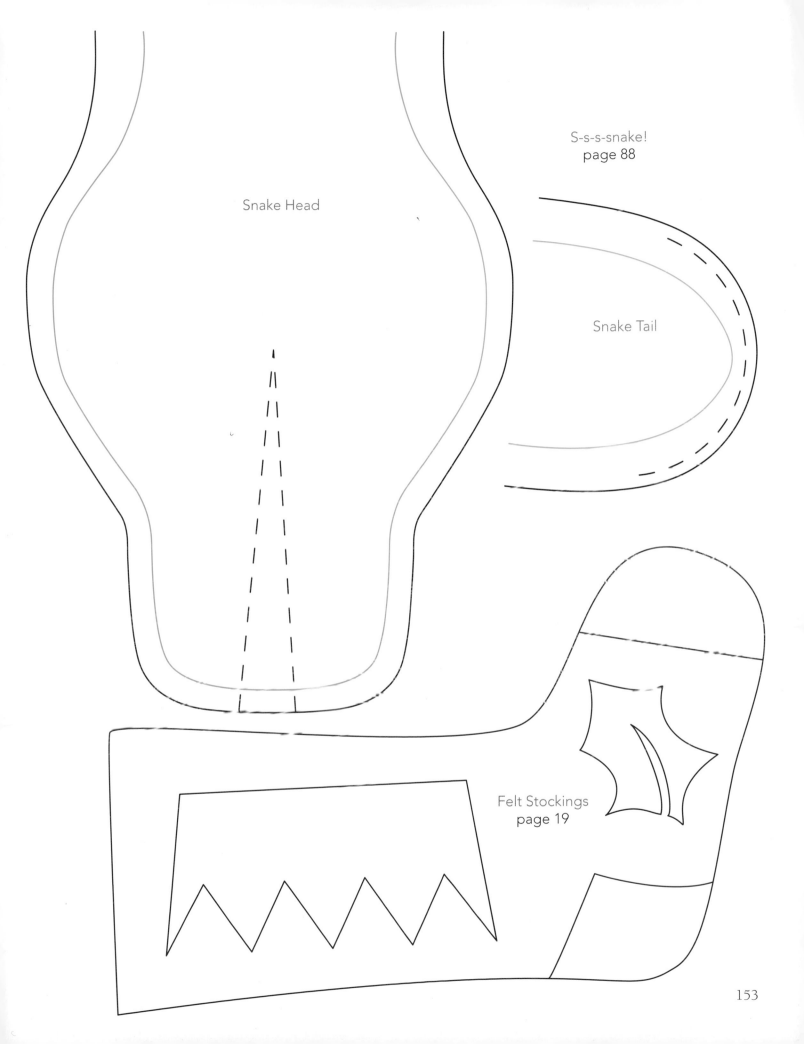

Snake Head

S-s-s-snake!
page 88

Snake Tail

Felt Stockings
page 19

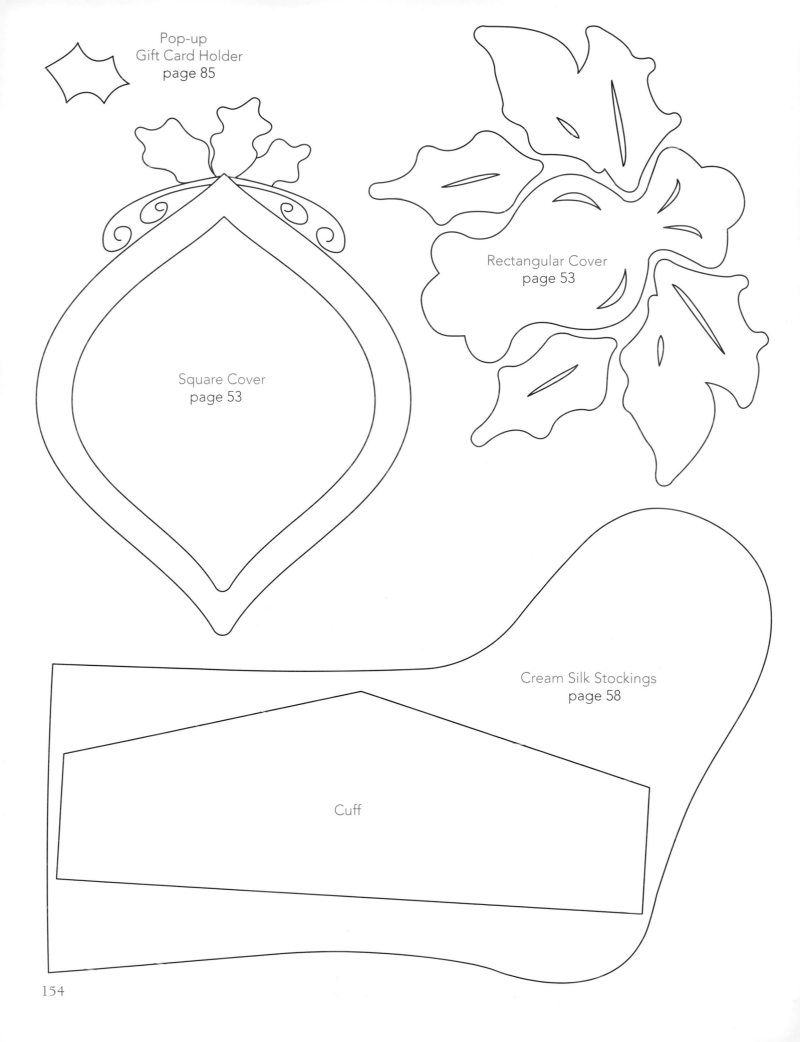

Pop-up
Gift Card Holder
page 85

Rectangular Cover
page 53

Square Cover
page 53

Cream Silk Stockings
page 58

Cuff

154

Welcome Mat
page 66

Holly Canvas
page 50

155

Apron Armhole

Apron Scallop

Apron Pocket

Scalloped Apron
page 92

Ornament
Gift Tag
page 96

Painted Plate
page 35

156

Recipe Index

157

Sizing Patterns

1. To change the size of a pattern, divide the desired height or width of the pattern (whichever is larger) by the actual height or width of the pattern. Multiply the result by 100 and photocopy the pattern at this percentage.

For example: You want your pattern to be 8" high, but the pattern on the page is 6" high. So 8 ÷ 6 = 1.33 x 100 = 133%. Copy the pattern at 133%.

2. If your copier doesn't enlarge to the size you need, enlarge the pattern to the maximum percentage on the copier. Then repeat step 1, dividing the desired size by the size of the enlarged pattern. Multiply this result by 100 and photocopy the enlarged pattern at the new percentage. (For very large projects, you'll need to enlarge the design in sections onto separate sheets of paper.) Repeat as needed to reach the desired size and tape the pattern pieces together.

Embroidery Stitches

Use three strands of embroidery floss for all stitches unless otherwise indicated in the project instructions. Follow the stitch diagrams to bring the needle up at odd numbers and down at even numbers.

French Knot

Running Stitch

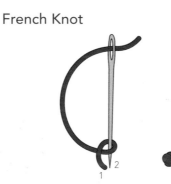

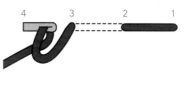

Cutting a Fabric Circle

Matching right sides, fold the fabric square in half from top to bottom and again from left to right. Tie one end of a length of string to a fabric pen; insert a thumbtack through the string at the length indicated in the project instructions. Insert the thumbtack through the folded corner of the fabric. Holding the tack in place and keeping the string taut, mark the cutting line (Fig. 1).

Fig. 1

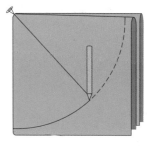

Fig. 2

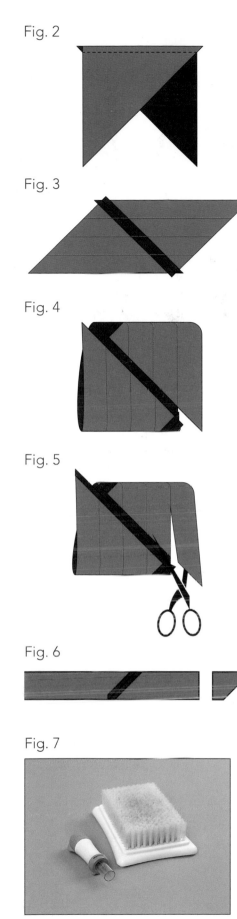

Fig. 3

Fig. 4

Fig. 5

Fig. 6

Continuous Bias Binding

1. Fold the fabric square in half diagonally; cut on the fold to make two triangles.
2. With right sides together and using a 1/4" seam allowance, sew the triangles together (Fig. 2). Press seam allowances open.
3. On the wrong side of the fabric, draw lines the width given in the project instructions, parallel to the long edges (Fig. 3). Cut off any remaining fabric less than this width.
4. With right sides inside, bring the short edges together to form a tube; match the raw edges so the first drawn line of the top section meets the second drawn line of the bottom section (Fig. 4).
5. Carefully pin the edges together by inserting pins through the drawn lines at the point where they intersect, making sure the pins go through the intersections on both sides. Using a 1/4" seam allowance, sew the edges together; press the seam allowances open.
6. To cut a continuous strip, begin cutting along the first drawn line (Fig. 5). Continue cutting along the drawn line around the tube.
7. Trim each end of the bias strip as shown in Fig. 6.

Needle Felting

Visit leisurearts.com to view a short needle felting Web cast.

Attach wool yarn to background fabric using a felting needle tool and mat (Fig. 7). Lightly punch the needles through the yarn and background fabric to interlock the fibers and join the pieces without sewing or gluing (Fig. 8). The brush-like mat allows the needles to easily pierce the fibers. We used the Clover Felting Needle Tool to make our projects—it has a locking plastic shield that provides protection from the sharp needles. Felt, wool, and woven cotton fabrics all work well as background fabrics.

Fig. 7

Fig. 8

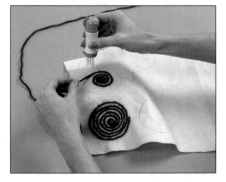

Credits

We offer our heartfelt thanks to these fine companies and gracious individuals.

For contributing their products for use in this book:

Plasteel Corporation for Dylite® foam shapes
Saral® Paper Corporation for transfer paper
The DMC Corporation for embroidery floss
Clover Needlecraft, Inc. for the felting needle tool and mat

For allowing us to photograph our projects in their homes:

Gary and Jane Bell

Jana Bishop

Stephen and Kim Hamblin

Margaret Kemp

Patricia Rhodes

Angela Simon

Randy and Anne Stocks

Kathe Sumbles

Linda Sunwall

Leighton Weeks

Ron and Becky Werle

Lawrence Young

For her delicious Curried Butternut Squash Soup recipe:

Maria E. Selig

And for their excellent photography:

Jason Masters

Ken West Photography